2

The language of maths

The School Mathematics Project

CAMBRIDGE
UNIVERSITY PRESS

Main authors	Stan Dolan
	Paul Roder
	Diana Sharvill
	Thelma Wilson
Contributions from	Ron Haydock
Team leader	Paul Roder

Published by the Press Syndicate of the University of Cambridge
The Pitt Building, Trumpington Street, Cambridge CB2 1RP
40 West 20th Street, New York, NY 10011–4211, USA
10 Stamford Road, Oakleigh, Melbourne 3166, Australia

© Cambridge University Press 1993

First published 1993

Produced by Gecko Limited, Bicester, Oxon.

Printed in Great Britain by Scotprint Ltd, Musselburgh

A catalogue record for this book is available from the British Library

Library of Congress cataloguing in publication data applied for

ISBN 0 521 44734 8

Cover photography by Tony Stone Images – Robert Frerck

Cover design by Iguana Creative Design

Notice to teachers

Contents

1 Straight-line graphs

1.1 Story graphs

Fun-fair rides like the one shown are found in many parts of the country. The ride is fun partly because of the almost violent changes of speed that you experience. Your body is not used to this type of motion.

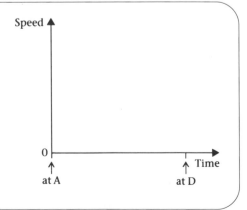

Imagine you are on the ride. Sketch a graph which shows how your speed changes with time as you go from A to D.

Do not worry about values on the axes for speed and time. Simply draw a graph which shows how you think the speed changes.

A graph gives you information. In a sense it tells a story. For example, the graph below shows what happened during a 100 m race between two girls on a school sports day.

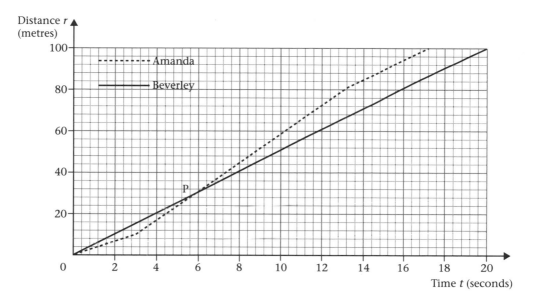

(a) Who won the race?

(b) What happened at the point labelled P on the graph?

(c) How fast was Beverley running?

(d) Amanda's speed changed during the race. Describe how her speed changed and compare it with Beverley's speed.

(e) In what way does the steepness of the graphs help you compare the speeds of the two girls?

(f) 'The formula $r = 5t$ describes Beverley's race.' Discuss what this statement means.

In this chapter you will learn how to interpret graphs, particularly linear (straight-line) graphs. You will also learn what a gradient is, how the gradient and intercept of a straight-line graph relate to the equation and how this knowledge can be used to find the equation of a **line of best fit.**

1.2 Linear graphs

Graphs are very important in mathematics. They can help you gain a
better understanding of formulas like the one in the discussion
point in section 1.1. A graph can make it possible to solve a problem
which would otherwise have been difficult. This chapter will
concentrate on formulas which give straight-line graphs. Formulas
which give curved graphs will be studied in chapter 5.

A straight-line graph is called a **linear graph**. A formula which
gives you a linear graph is called a **linear equation**. For
example:

$$y = 4 + 2x$$

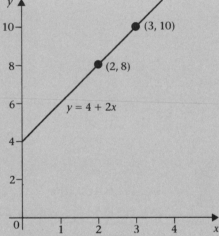

You can plot the graph of a linear equation if you know **at
least two** points which fit the equation. For example:

x	y
2	8
3	10

You can find the coordinates of a point by **substituting** a
value for x (or y) in the equation. For example, if:

$$x = 3 \quad \text{then} \quad y = 4 + 2 \times 3 = 10$$

You can plot a linear graph if you know at least two points.
Why is it advisable to plot at least three points?

EXAMPLE 1

Draw a graph of $y = \frac{1}{2}x + 1$ for x-values from 0 to 10.

SOLUTION

To find three points on the graph for values of x from 0 to 10, choose three x-values in this range (for example, $x = 0$, 6 and 10) and find the corresponding y-values.

x	y
0	1
6	4
10	6

A scale which has x from 0 to 10 and y from 0 to 6 will enable you to plot all three points.

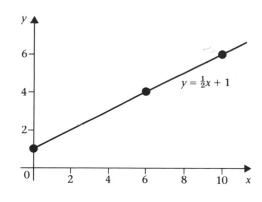

EXERCISE 1

1 (a) If $y = \frac{1}{2}x$ find y when:

(i) $x = 4$ (ii) $x = 10$ (iii) $x = 0$

(b) Use your answers to (a) to plot the points $(0, \underline{\hspace{0.3cm}})$, $(4, \underline{\hspace{0.3cm}})$ and $(10, \underline{\hspace{0.3cm}})$. Join up the points with a straight line and so draw the graph of $y = \frac{1}{2}x$. (If the result is not a straight line, you must have made a mistake!)

2 (a) On a piece of graph paper, draw axes from $x = 0$ to 10 and from $y = {}^{-}5$ to 10.

(b) Use the method of question 1 to draw graphs for the following equations:

(i) $y = \frac{1}{2}x$ (ii) $y = 3 + \frac{1}{2}x$ (iii) $y = \frac{1}{2}x - 3$

(c) In what way are the graphs similar?

1.3 Gradient

Gradient is a measure of steepness.

Gradient $= \frac{2}{10}$
$= 0{\cdot}2$
$= 20\%$

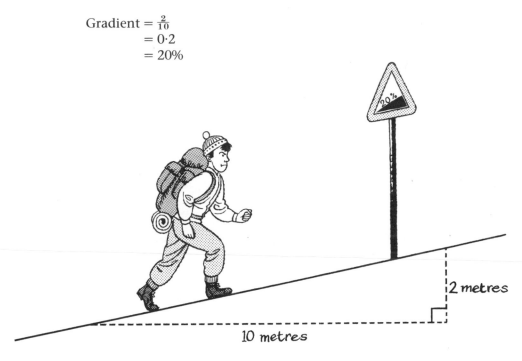

The steepness of a graph can often give you useful information. In section 1.1, for example, you saw that the graph of the race for Amanda was steeper than that for Beverley for much of the race. This showed that Amanda was running faster than Beverley.

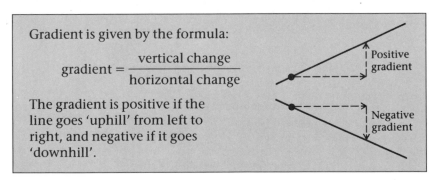

Gradient is given by the formula:

$$\text{gradient} = \frac{\text{vertical change}}{\text{horizontal change}}$$

The gradient is positive if the line goes 'uphill' from left to right, and negative if it goes 'downhill'.

Positive gradient

Negative gradient

(a) Describe a line which has zero gradient.

(b) Does a vertical line have a gradient?

EXAMPLE 2

What is the gradient of the line joining (0, 8) and (5, 0)?

SOLUTION

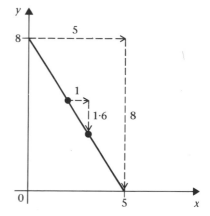

The gradient is negative since it goes 'downhill' from left to right.

For every 5 units it goes along, it goes down 8.

So it goes down $\frac{8}{5} = 1.6$ for every 1 it goes along.

The gradient is ⁻1.6.

EXERCISE 2

1 Which of the following lines have a positive gradient and which have a negative gradient?

(a)   (b)   (c)

(d)   (e)   (f)

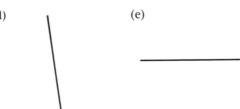

2 What is the gradient of the line joining the following pairs of points? (You may find it helpful to plot the points on a grid.)

(a) (2, 7), (5, 10)   (b) (2, 7), (6, 5)

(c) (4, 1), (⁻2, 10)   (d) (⁻1, 5), (4, 5)

(e) (1·2, 3·6), (3·7, 7·2)   (f) (⁻2·3, 3·0), (0·5, 5·7)

1.4 Gradients and intercepts

The look of a graph can be deceptive. A steep gradient can be made to look less steep by changing the scale of the axes. For example, both the graphs shown below have a gradient of 2.

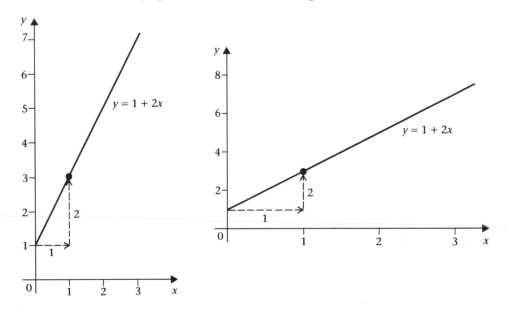

The graph of a linear equation can be drawn if you know two points. You can also draw the graph if you know the gradient of the line and the point where the line cuts the y-axis. This is called the **y-intercept** of the graph.

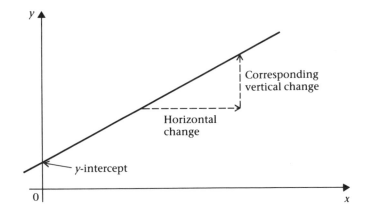

 TASKSHEET 1 — y = c + mx (page 13)

1.5 Lines of best fit

Knowing the relationship between the gradient, the intercept and the formula defining a linear graph is particularly useful when you need to find a formula for a **line of best fit** for experimental data.

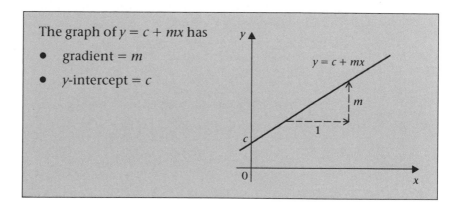

The graph of $y = c + mx$ has

- gradient $= m$
- y-intercept $= c$

TASKSHEET 2 — Lines of best fit (page 15)

EXAMPLE 3

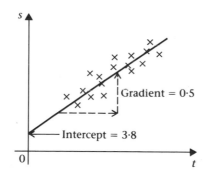

A line of best fit was drawn through a set of points plotted from data collected during an experiment.

(a) What is the equation of a line of best fit if the gradient is 0·5 and the intercept is 3·8?

(b) What value for s would you expect when t is equal to 2?

SOLUTION

(a) In this case, the variables are s and t rather than y and x so you need an equation of the form $s = c + mt$.

The gradient is 0·5 so $m = 0·5$.

The intercept is 3·8 so $c = 3·8$.

Therefore the equation of the graph is $s = 3·8 + 0·5t$.

(b) When $t = 2$,
$$s = 3·8 + 0·5 \times 2 = 4·8$$

11

After working through this chapter, you should:

1   know what a linear equation is and how to draw its straight-line graph;

2   appreciate what is meant by the gradient and the intercept of a straight-line graph;

3   know how the gradient and intercept of a linear graph relate to its equation;

4   be able to find the equation of a line of best fit.

$y = c + mx$

The gradient and intercept of a straight-line graph can be found from its equation. This tasksheet shows you how.

First calculate the y-intercept by calculating y when x is zero.

For example, if $y = 5 - 3x$ then putting $x = 0$ gives:

$$y = 5 - 3 \times 0$$
$$= 5 - 0$$
$$= 5$$

So the intercept is $y = 5$.

To calculate the gradient you need one other point. You know the graph passes through $(0, 5)$ so it is sensible to find y when $x = 1$.

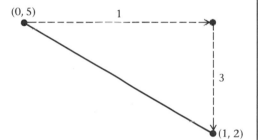

If you put $x = 1$ you find that:

$$y = 5 - 3 \times 1$$
$$= 5 - 3$$
$$= 2$$

So the graph passes through $(1, 2)$.

The line slopes downhill, so the gradient of the line joining $(0, 5)$ and $(1, 2)$ is:

$$\frac{^-3}{1} = {}^-3$$

1 Copy and complete the tables shown below.

Equation	Intercept	Gradient
$y = 5 + \frac{1}{2}x$		
$y = 5 + x$		
$y = 5 + 2x$		
$y = 5 + 3x$		

Equation	Intercept	Gradient
$y = 5 - \frac{1}{2}x$		
$y = 5 - x$		
$y = 5 - 2x$		
$y = 5 - 3x$		

2 Describe the effect of increasing or decreasing the value of m on the graph of $y = 5 + mx$. (You may find it helpful to plot the equations from question 1 on a graph plotter.)

3 Copy and complete the tables shown below.

Equation	Intercept	Gradient
$y = 1 + x$		
$y = 2 + x$		
$y = 3 + x$		

Equation	Intercept	Gradient
$y = {}^-1 + x$		
$y = {}^-2 + x$		
$y = {}^-3 + x$		

4 Describe the effect of increasing or decreasing the value of c on the graph of $y = c + x$. (You may find it helpful to use a graph plotter to plot the graphs of the equations from question 3.)

5 Copy and complete the table shown below. (You do not have to **calculate** the gradients and intercepts; simply write down what you think they are.)

Equation	Intercept	Gradient
$y = 5 - 3x$	5	$^-3$
$y = 5 + 3x$		
$y = {}^-3 + 2x$		
$y = 3 - x$		
$y = 2 \cdot 5 + 1 \cdot 5x$		

6 Use a graph plotter to draw the graphs of the equations given in question 5 and check that the intercepts and gradients found in question 5 agree with the graphs you get.

7 For the graph of the general linear equation $y = c + mx$, what is represented by:

(a) c (b) m

Lines of best fit

Choose one of the two experiments described below. In each case collect data, plot the data as points on a graph and draw a line of best fit (a straight line which passes near to as many points as possible). Then make a note of the intercept and calculate the gradient of the line. (Take care to read the scale and do not just count squares!) Hence write down the equation of the line of best fit. Also try to describe what **meaning** can be given to the gradient and intercept.

EXPERIMENT 1

Roll a ball down a ramp onto a track made from two metre rules. (Remember always to start from the same point on the ramp each time you do the experiment.) Measure the time, t seconds, it takes the ball to travel a distance, s centimetres, along the track. Do this for various values of s.

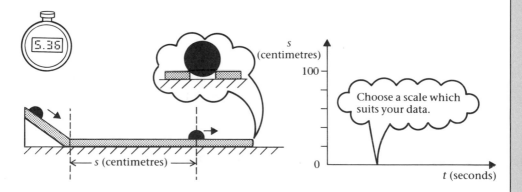

EXPERIMENT 2

Choose a group of students of various ages from your school. Measure each student's height and also note his or her age.

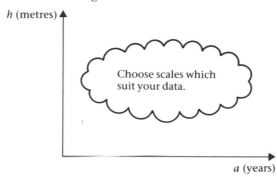

15

2 Graphs and equations

2.1 Brenda's Boats

Suppose you are on holiday near a river and find two companies,
Alan's Boat-yard and Brenda's Boats, who hire out boats by the hour.
Alan charges £3 per hour while Brenda has a £4 standing charge in
addition to charging £2 per hour. Brenda's charges are on this graph.

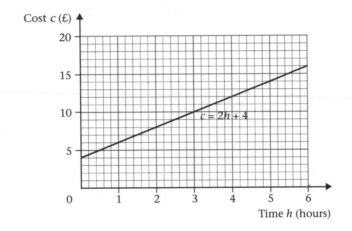

(a) Check that Brenda's graph gives the correct charge for:

(i) 2 hours; (ii) 3 hours; (iii) 4 hours;

(iv) 5 hours.

(b) Explain how the formula $c = 2h + 4$ can be used to
calculate the charge, £c for h hours, for Brenda's Boats.

(c) Copy the graph for Brenda's charges onto graph paper.
Draw a graph on the same axes to show Alan's charges.

(d) What formula would you use to describe Alan's graph?

(e) Why is Alan's graph steeper than Brenda's?

(f) Find the coordinates of the point where the two graphs
cross. What is special about this point?

(g) If you have a £20 voucher to spend at Brenda's Boats, for
how many hours can you hire a boat? (Explain carefully
how you worked out your answer.)

2.2 **Solving equations**

In the previous section, you saw that Brenda's Boats charges according to the formula:

$$c = 2h + 4$$

where c is the charge in pounds and h is the time in hours.

Suppose you want to hire a boat for as long as possible. You have only £11 to spend and you want to know for how long you can hire a boat. Brenda writes down the following equation:

$$2h + 4 = 11$$

An equation is an algebraic statement with a left-hand side (LHS) **equal** to a right-hand side (RHS). Here, the LHS is $2h + 4$ and the RHS is 11. The two sides of an equation are said to be **balanced** and it is helpful to think of them as the loads in the two pans of a balance.

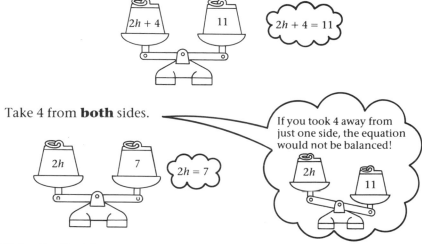

Take 4 from **both** sides.

If you took 4 away from just one side, the equation would not be balanced!

Halve **both** sides.

You can hire a boat for $3\frac{1}{2}$ hours.

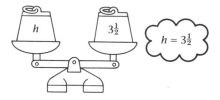

Write down and solve the equation to determine for how long you can hire a boat for £14.

Apart from adding and subtracting numbers to solve an equation, you may need to add or subtract an algebraic expression. This is not a problem if you remember that x just stands for a number that you are trying to find. For example, you know that:

$$5 \times 4 - 2 \times 4 = 3 \times 4 \quad \text{because} \quad 20 - 8 = 12$$
$$\text{and} \quad 5 \times 7 - 2 \times 7 = 3 \times 7 \quad \text{because} \quad 35 - 14 = 21$$

In general:

$$5x - 2x = 3x \quad \text{for any number } x$$

This result is used in the next example.

EXAMPLE 1

Solve the equation $5x - 7 = 2x + 8$.

SOLUTION

$$
\begin{aligned}
5x - 7 &= 2x + 8 \\
5x &= 2x + 15 \qquad &&\text{(Add 7 to \textbf{both} sides.)} \\
3x &= 15 \qquad &&\text{(Subtract } 2x \text{ from \textbf{both} sides.)} \\
x &= 5 \qquad &&\text{(Divide \textbf{both} sides by 3.)}
\end{aligned}
$$

Check that $5x - 7$ does in fact equal $2x + 8$ when $x = 5$.

EXERCISE 1

1 Solve the following equations:

   (a) $3x + 7 = 34$ (b) $17 = 2x - 3$

   (c) $\frac{1}{3}x + 5 = 15$ (d) $5x + 1{\cdot}4 = 7{\cdot}6$

2 Simplify the following expressions:

   (a) $3x + 5x - 2x$ (b) $4x + 17 - x + 3$

3 Solve the following equations:

   (a) $7x - 5 = 3x + 27$ (b) $x + 5 = 41 - 3x$

2.3 The point of intersection

In section 2.1, the point where the graphs crossed was important because it showed you the hiring time for which the two boat-yards would charge the same. There are many similar situations where it is helpful to find where two graphs intersect.

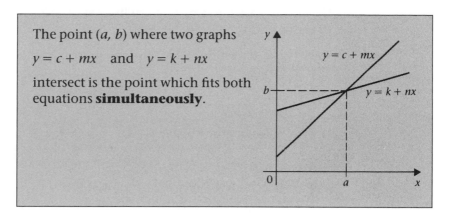

The point (a, b) where two graphs

$y = c + mx$ and $y = k + nx$

intersect is the point which fits both equations **simultaneously**.

E X A M P L E 2

Show that the point (4, 12) fits both $y = 4 + 2x$ and $y = 24 - 3x$ simultaneously.

S O L U T I O N

For equation $y = 4 + 2x$, when $x = 4$, $y = 4 + 2 \times 4 = 12$.
For equation $y = 24 - 3x$, when $x = 4$, $y = 24 - 3 \times 4 = 12$.
$x = 4$ and $y = 12$ fit **both** equations.

Draw the graphs of $y = 4 + 2x$ and $y = 24 - 3x$ on graph paper (or use a graph plotter) and check that they intersect at the point (4, 12).

This thinking point suggest a graphical approach to finding the point of intersection. An alternative approach is to **calculate** the values of x and y by solving equations. Such an algebraic method is illustrated in the next example.

E X A M P L E   3

Find the point of intersection of $y = 4 + 2x$ and $y = 24 - 3x$.

S O L U T I O N

The y-values are the same on both lines at the point of intersection.
So at this point, $4 + 2x = 24 - 3x$.

$$4 + 2x = 24 - 3x \quad \text{(Add } 3x \text{ to both sides.)}$$
$$4 + 5x = 24 \quad \text{(Subtract 4 from both sides.)}$$
$$5x = 20 \quad \text{(Divide both sides by 5.)}$$
$$x = 4$$

The two lines intersect when $x = 4$.

Either equation can now be used to find the y-value.

$y = 4 + 2x$ and $x = 4$ give $y = 4 + 2 \times 4 = 12$.

The point of intersection is (4, 12).

(The other equation can be used as a check. In this case,
$24 - 3 \times 4 = 12$ confirms the answer as (4, 12).)

E X E R C I S E   2

1 Find the point of intersection for each of these pairs of lines.

(a) $y = 4x - 12$ (b) $y = 2x - 1$ (c) $y = \frac{1}{2}x + 2$
      $y = x + 3$ $y = x - 8$ $y = 11 - x$

(Check your answers on a graph plotter.)

2 The following three lines make a
triangle.

$$y = 5x - 15$$
$$y = 45 - x$$
$$y = 9 + 0 \cdot 2x$$

Find the coordinates of the
corners of the triangle.

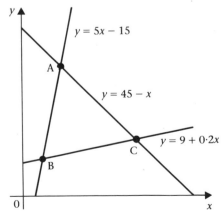

2.4 Simultaneous equations

Brenda sells ice-cream at her boat-yard. She sells small and large cones. One afternoon she has only two customers. One buys three small and four large cones. The other buys one small and two large cones.

Small cones	Large cones	Total cost
3	4	£4·00
1	2	£1·80

There is enough information here for you to puzzle out how much each of the ice-creams costs. The tasksheet will show you a way of solving this type of problem.

TASKSHEET 1 — Simultaneous equations (page 25)

The problem of the cost of ice-creams can be solved using algebra.

You have two unknown quantities, the cost of a small cone and the cost of a large cone.

Let a small cone cost x pence and a large cone cost y pence.

So $\quad 3x + 4y = 400$
and $\quad x + 2y = 180$

> Explain why $3x + 4y = 400$.

Doubling the second equation gives:

$$2x + 4y = 360$$

The difference between this and the equation for the first customer's order gives the value of x.

$$
\begin{array}{l}
3x + 4y = 400 \\
2x + 4y = 360 \\
\hline
x \qquad = 40 \qquad \text{A small cone costs 40p.}
\end{array}
$$

Substituting $x = 40$ into the equation $x + 2y = 180$:

$$
\begin{aligned}
40 + 2y &= 180 \\
2y &= 140 \\
y &= 70 \qquad \text{A large cone costs 70p.}
\end{aligned}
$$

21

This method of solving the problem is called **solving simultaneous equations by elimination**. Where you have two unknown quantities and two different linear equations it is always possible to eliminate one of the unknowns by adding or subtracting equations. When you have found one of the quantities you can then find the other by substituting back into one of your two equations.

E X A M P L E 4

Solve the simultaneous equations:

$$2x + \quad y = 18$$
$$x + 3y = 19$$

SOLUTION

There are two ways of solving these simultaneous equations by elimination. You could choose to eliminate x to find y, or you could eliminate y and so find x.

(a) To eliminate x you need the same number of xs in each equation. Doubling the second equation gives $2x + 6y = 38$ and subtracting the first equation from this eliminates all the x-values.

$$2x + 6y = 38$$
$$2x + \quad y = 18$$
$$\overline{ 5y = 20} \qquad \text{so } y = 4$$

Substituting $y = 4$ into either of the equations gives $x = 7$.

(b) To eliminate y you need the same number of ys in each equation. Multiplying the first equation by 3 gives $6x + 3y = 54$ and subtracting the second equation from this eliminates all the y-values.

$$6x + 3y = 54$$
$$x + 3y = 19$$
$$\overline{5x \qquad = 35} \qquad \text{so } x = 7$$

Substituting $x = 7$ into either of the equations gives $y = 4$.

Both methods give $x = 7$ and $y = 4$ as the solution to the simultaneous equations. (Although you only need to use one of these methods to obtain a solution, you should always substitute both values into **both** of your original equations to check your solution.)

EXERCISE 3

1 (a) Solve the simultaneous equations:
$$x + y = 17$$
$$2x + y = 31$$

(b) Use a graph plotter to find the point of intersection of the graphs of $y = 17 - x$ and $y = 31 - 2x$.

(c) Explain the connection between your answers to (a) and (b).

2 Solve the following simultaneous equations.

(a) $4x + 2y = 10$
$x + 2y = 7$

(b) $3x + y = 12$
$3x + 2y = 15$

3

Harry's Hamburgers sells hot dogs as well as hamburgers. Harry asks his assistant to keep a record of what is sold to each customer together with the cost.

Hot dogs	Hamburgers	Total cost
2	3	£2·55
1	4	£2·65
3	3	£3·00
2	1	£1·55
3	2	£2·45

(a) The first two entries are correct. Use this information to calculate the prices of hot dogs and hamburgers.

(b) The assistant made a mistake in calculating the total cost of one of the remaining three entries. Find out which one is wrong and correct the error.

23

4 Solve the following simultaneous equations:

(a) $3x + 2y = 24$
$2x + y = 15$

(b) $3x + 5y = 31$
$2x + 3y = 20$

After working through this chapter, you should:

1 appreciate how to simplify equations whilst keeping them in balance;

2 be able to solve linear equations;

3 appreciate the relationship between points of intersection and the solution of simultaneous equations;

4 know how to solve simultaneous linear equations.

Simultaneous equations

Let represent a small cone and let represent a large cone.

Suppose you know that:

   +   cost 400p ①

 +   cost 180p ②

1 Explain why:

  +   cost 360p ③

2 Explain, using ① and ③, why you can deduce that 1 small cone must cost 40p.

3 Show how you can calculate the cost of a large cone.

4 2 hot dogs and 1 hamburger cost 150p.

  (a) What would 4 hot dogs and 2 hamburgers cost?

  (b) What would 10 hot dogs and 5 hamburgers cost?

5 (a) If, in addition, 4 hot dogs and 5 hamburgers cost 390p, explain:

   (i) how you can use your answer to 4(a) to calculate the cost of 3 hamburgers;

   (ii) how you can use your answer to 4(b) to calculate the cost of 6 hot dogs.

  (b) What is the cost of 1 hamburger?

  (c) What is the cost of 1 hot dog?

3 Sequences

3.1 Number patterns

A sequence is a list of numbers connected by some rule. Spotting a pattern usually allows you to work out what the rule is and so continue the sequence.

(a) What are the next two terms in the sequence

4, 7, 10, 13, . . . ?

(b) Describe carefully what pattern allows you to continue listing the sequence.

T A S K S H E E T   1   —   Simple sequences (page 34)

Sometimes a sequence of spatial arrangements can lead to a sequence of numbers.

Here, the number of matchsticks needed to make connected squares leads to the sequence 4, 7, 10, 13, . . .

(a) Write down a number sequence for each of the spatial arrangements below.

(i)

(ii)

(b) Describe the spatial arrangements and explain how you can continue the number sequences.

Suppose the first stage of a tennis tournament is a round robin; that is, everyone in the group plays everyone else just once. It is the organiser's job to work out how many matches need to be played.

(a) How many matches altogether need to be played for the 5 competitors shown in the picture?

(b) How many matches need to be played if there are:

(i) 2   (ii) 3   (iii) 4

competitors in a group?

(c) Write the number of matches needed as a number sequence and explain how the sequence can be continued.

(d) Where have you seen this sequence before?

EXERCISE 1

1 Find the next two terms in each sequence. Write down what you think the tenth term will be.

(a) 28, 25, 22, 19, 16, . . .

(b) 1, 4, 9, 16, . . .

(c) 3, 7, 11, 15, . . .

(d) 1, 3, 6, 10, 15, . . .

(e) $\frac{1}{2}, \frac{2}{3}, \frac{3}{4}, \frac{4}{5}, \ldots$

2 Draw a spatial arrangement for each of the following sequences.

(a) 2, 4, 6, 8, 10, . . .

(b) 1, 8, 27, 64, . . .

(c) $\frac{1}{2}, \frac{2}{3}, \frac{3}{4}, \frac{4}{5}, \ldots$

3.2 Further sequences

A customer is haggling over the price of a rug in a Greek market. The trader starts by asking for 6000 drachmas. The customer offers 2000 drachmas. The trader halves the difference, asking for 4000 drachmas, which is the average of 6000 and 2000 drachmas. The customer then offers the average of 2000 and 4000 drachmas, which is 3000 drachmas. They continue to haggle in this way.

The sequence of bids 6000, 2000, 4000, 3000, . . . is different from previous sequences in this chapter because each term depends on the previous **two** terms.

(a) What are the next two terms in the sequence? (In other words, what will be the next bid by the trader and the next offer from the customer?)

(b) What difference would it make if the customer started the bidding? (Write down the first six terms of the sequence.)

Perhaps the best-known sequence of the type where each term is related to the previous two terms is the **Fibonacci sequence**, named after Leonardo Fibonacci, who discovered its importance.

The Fibonacci sequence is:

   1, 1, 2, 3, 5, 8, 13, . . .

Each term is the sum of the previous two terms.

   $1 + 1 = 2$, $1 + 2 = 3$, $2 + 3 = 5$, $3 + 5 = 8$, $5 + 8 = 13$, . . .

In section 3.1 you saw that the sequence of numbers associated with dots arranged in triangular patterns was the same as that obtained when calculating the number of matches needed in a round robin tournament. It is often the case that a particular sequence of numbers is related to several quite different situations and this is particularly true for the Fibonacci sequence. Many patterns in nature appear to relate to this sequence.

An example of Fibonacci numbers occurring in nature is shown in the diagram. In many plants, the way in which the leaves are arranged round the stem follows a pattern.

The number of leaves between any leaf and the one directly above it depends on the type of plant, but for different types of plant this number is one of 1, 2, 3, 5, 8, . . ., the numbers in the Fibonacci sequence.

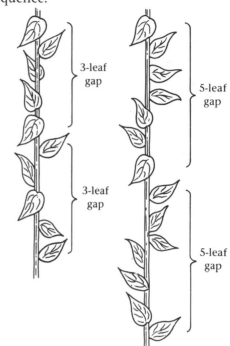

EXERCISE 2

1   Work out the next two terms in these sequences.

(a) $\frac{1}{2}, \frac{1}{3}, \frac{2}{5}, \frac{3}{8}, \frac{5}{13}, \ldots$

(b) 2, 10, 6, 8, 7, . . .

(c) 0, 2, 2, 4, 6, 10, . . .

2   In a market, the trader asks a first price of 4000 drachmas and the customer makes a first offer of 2000 drachmas. Each subsequent bid is the average of the two previous bids. Work out the next five bids if:

(a) the trader starts,

(b) the customer starts.

If you were the trader, would you try to start the bidding? Explain your answer.

3.3 The general term

To find later terms in a sequence it may be easier to use a rule which relates the terms of a sequence to the counting numbers.

Counting numbers	1	2	3	4	...		r		...
Sequence		4	7	10	13	...	rth term		...

To find the general rule for this sequence, think back to the arrangement of matchsticks. Think of the squares like this:

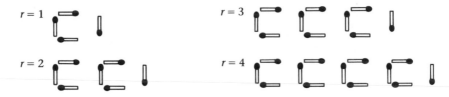

Explain why this shows that the rth term is $3r + 1$.

To find the 50th term there is no need to find the previous 49 terms. The 50th term will be $3 \times 50 + 1 = 151$.

If you know an expression for the general term of a sequence, any term can be found by substitution in that expression.

EXAMPLE 1

The expression for the rth term of a sequence is:

$$\frac{r}{2r + 1}$$

Write down the first five terms and the 50th term.

SOLUTION

Substituting the numbers 1, 2, 3, 4, 5 and 50 for r gives:

$$\frac{1}{3}, \frac{2}{5}, \frac{3}{7}, \frac{4}{9}, \frac{5}{11}, \cdots \frac{50}{101}$$

For some sequences, you may be able to find an expression for the general term by comparing the terms with those of a well-known sequence such as the counting numbers or the triangle numbers.

E X A M P L E 2

Find the next term of the sequence:

5, 9, 13, 17, 21, . . .

Find an expression for the general term and so calculate the 50th term.

S O L U T I O N

Each term is four more than the previous term, so the sixth term will be 25.

The fact that each term is four more than the previous one gives a clue to help find the general term.

Counting numbers	1	2	3	4	5	. . .	r	. . .
Counting numbers ×4	4	8	12	16	20	. . .	$4r$	. . .
Sequence	5	9	13	17	21	. . .	$4r + 1$	. . .

The rth term is $4r + 1$, so the expression for the general term is $4r + 1$.

To find the 50th term, substitute 50 into the expression for the general term to give $4 \times 50 + 1 = 201$.

T A S K S H E E T 2 – *Using the general term (page 35)*

You have met these sequences already:

- counting numbers: 1, 2, 3, 4, 5, . . . , r, . . .
- square numbers: 1, 4, 9, 16, 25, . . . , r^2, . . .
- cube numbers: 1, 8, 27, 64, 125, . . . , r^3, . . .
- triangle numbers: 1, 3, 6, 10, 15, . . . , $\dfrac{r(r + 1)}{2}$, . . .

Relate this sequence to the square numbers and find an expression for the general term.

2, 5, 10, 17, 26, . . .

E X E R C I S E 3

1 Write down the first five terms for each sequence. The rth term is given in each case.

   (a) $2r - 1$

   (b) r^3

   (c) $2r^2 - 1$

   (d) $\dfrac{r - 1}{r + 1}$

2 Find an expression for the number of dots in the rth term of each sequence.

   (a)

   (b)

3 Find an expression for the rth term for each sequence.

   (a) $2, 4, 6, 8, \ldots$

   (b) $3, 5, 7, 9, \ldots$

   (c) $5, 11, 17, 23, 29, \ldots$

   (d) $\frac{1}{2}, \frac{2}{3}, \frac{3}{4}, \frac{4}{5}, \ldots$

After working through this chapter you should:

1 understand what a sequence is;

2 know the particular sequences:

- counting numbers: $1, 2, 3, 4, 5, \ldots, r, \ldots$

- square numbers: $1, 4, 9, 16, 25, \ldots, r^2, \ldots$

- cube numbers: $1, 8, 27, 64, 125, \ldots, r^3, \ldots$

- triangle numbers: $1, 3, 6, 10, 15, \ldots, \dfrac{r(r+1)}{2}, \ldots$

- Fibonacci sequence: $1, 1, 2, 3, 5, 8, 13, \ldots$;

3 be able to find the general term of a simple sequence;

4 know how to use a flow chart and/or write a short program to generate a sequence.

Simple sequences

The numbers in a sequence are known as the terms.

1 Follow the instructions in this flow chart to write down ten terms in a sequence.

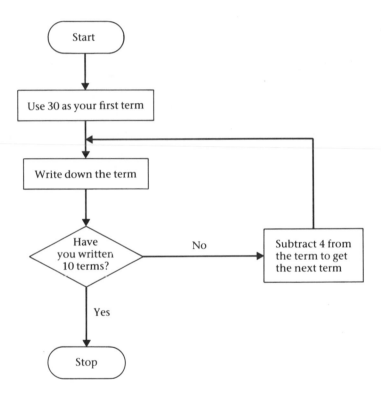

2 Draw a flow chart which would give the sequence:

3, 5, 7, 9, 11, ... , 21

3E Write a set of instructions for a programmable calculator or computer to produce the sequence of the first eight multiples of 5.

Using the general term

1 (a) Work through the following two flow charts.

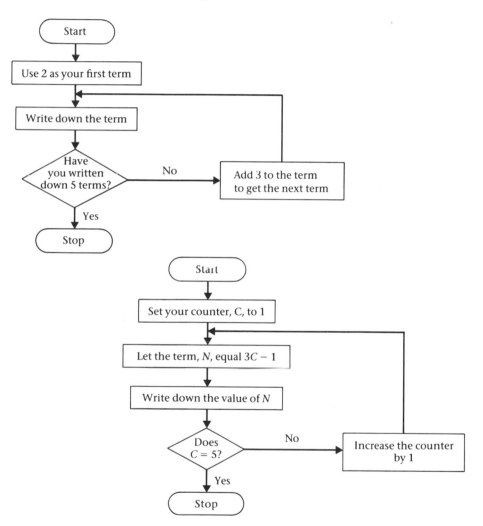

(b) What do you notice about the two sequences produced in (a)?

2E Write two different sets of programming instructions which would produce the sequence:

1, 5, 9, 13, 17

3 Work through the following flow charts.

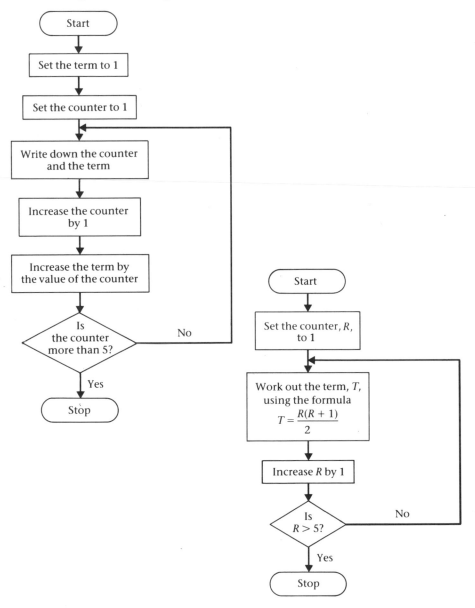

4E Use the flow charts from question 3 to write two different sets of programming instructions to produce the first five triangle numbers.

Formulas and inequalities

4.1 Formulas

Paul was cooking some biscuits. The instructions in his cookery book were to put them in an oven at 300° for about 10 minutes. He followed the recipe but found that his biscuits were burnt and inedible.

He then realised that his cookery book gave all temperatures in °F, while his oven was marked in °C.

The conversion formula, $F = 1 \cdot 8C + 32$, can be used to change between °F and °C.

For the biscuits, $F = 300$, so $300 = 1 \cdot 8C + 32$.

At what temperature, in °C, should Paul have set his oven?

Paul wants to continue to use his book, but all its recipes give the oven temperature in °F. He therefore decides that it will be sensible to rearrange the conversion formula to the form:

$C = \ldots$

C would then be called the **subject** of the formula.

The conversion formula can be written in a flow diagram.

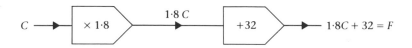

By reversing the flow diagram, C can be made the subject of the formula.

$$\frac{F - 32}{1 \cdot 8} \longleftarrow \boxed{\div 1 \cdot 8} \xleftarrow{\quad F - 32 \quad} \boxed{-32} \longleftarrow F$$

So $C = \dfrac{F - 32}{1 \cdot 8}$

37

(a) Use the formula $C = \dfrac{F - 32}{1 \cdot 8}$ to find C when $F = 300$ and check that your answer agrees with the one you obtained at the beginning of this section.

(b) When reversing the flow diagram for $F = 1 \cdot 8C + 32$, the first operation was $- 32$.

$- 32$ has the opposite effect to $+ 32$. It is known as the **inverse operation** to $+ 32$.

What was the inverse operation to $\times 1 \cdot 8$?

(c) What is the inverse operation to:

(i) $- 54$; (ii) $\div 4$?

(d) To work out F from $F = 1 \cdot 8C + 32$, you first multiply by $1 \cdot 8$ and then add 32. What happens to the order when you reverse the flow diagram?

(e) Use flow diagrams to make b the subject of each of these formulas:

(i) $a = \tfrac{1}{2}b - 5$ (ii) $a = \dfrac{b - 4}{3}$

You may prefer to draw balance diagrams rather than flow diagrams to change the subject of the formula.

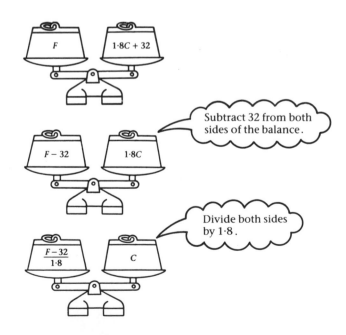

Subtract 32 from both sides of the balance.

Divide both sides by $1 \cdot 8$.

> Use balance diagrams to make x the subject of $y = \dfrac{x + 5}{4}$

When changing the subject of a formula, it may be sensible to draw either a flow diagram or balance diagrams. With experience, you may find that you can leave out the balance and simply write:

$$F = 1 \cdot 8C + 32$$
$$F - 32 = 1 \cdot 8C$$
$$\frac{F - 32}{1 \cdot 8} = C$$

EXERCISE 1

1 A label on a pack of beef states that the cooking time is 40 minutes per kilogram plus an extra 30 minutes. This can be written as $T = 40W + 30$.

  (a) How long does it take to cook a 2 kg piece of meat?

  (b) Rearrange the formula to make W the subject.

  (c) What weight of meat will be cooked in 3 hours 10 minutes?

2 Make a the subject of each of these formulas:

  (a) $u = 7a - 6$ (b) $V = \dfrac{a - 5}{2}$ (c) $B = \frac{1}{3}a + c$

3 To work out $\frac{4}{5}$ of a number, you divide it by 5 and then multiply by 4. Use this idea to make a the subject of each of these formulas:

  (a) $H = \frac{4}{5}a + c$ (b) $y = \frac{2}{3}a - 3$

4 A mini-enterprise group prints leaflets. It offers two scales of charges:
A: standing charge of £2 plus 5p per leaflet;
B: standing charge of £4 plus 3p per leaflet.

  (a) Explain why the formula for the charge on scale A can be written as $C = 200 + 5N$, if N is the number of leaflets printed and C is the cost in pence.

  (b) Rearrange this formula to make N the subject.

  (c) Write down the formula for scale B and then make N the subject of that formula.

  (d) Which scale would give you more leaflets for £10?

5E (a) Make u the subject of the formula $v = u + at$.

  (b) Make a the subject of the formula $v = u + at$.

4.2 **Inequalities**

Jan hires out boats at £4 per hour plus a standing charge of £5.

> (a) If Kaljinder and Kaljeet spend £17 on hiring the boat for *n* hours, explain why $17 = 4n + 5$.
>
> (b) For how long did they hire the boat?

Andy and Bob have £25 which they can spend on hiring a boat. If they hire the boat for *n* hours, then $4n + 5$ must be less than or equal to 25. You can write this as:

$$4n + 5 \leqslant 25$$

They cannot hire the boat for parts of an hour, so *n* must be a whole number.

> (a) Can Andy and Bob hire the boat for:
>
>   (i) 4 hours;   (ii) 5 hours;   (iii) 6 hours?
>
> (b) Write down all the possible solutions to $4n + 5 \leqslant 25$, remembering that *n* can only be a whole number.
>
> (d) Ron and Diana spend **more than** £30. Write down the inequality which describes this and give three possible values for *n*.

EXAMPLE 1

Stan's Boats charge £13 plus £7 per hour to hire a motor boat. Jo decides to spend between £30 and £50.

(a) Write down the inequality for the number of hours, *n*, for which the boat can be hired.

(b) What hiring times are possible if the boat can be hired for whole hours and half hours?

(c) Use a number line to show the possible hiring times.

SOLUTION

(a) The inequality is $30 \leqslant 7n + 13 \leqslant 50$.

(b) First solve $7n + 13 = 30$ and $7n + 13 = 50$

$$7n = 17 \qquad\qquad 7n = 37$$

$$n = 17 \div 7 = 2\cdot43 \qquad\qquad n = 37 \div 7 = 5\cdot29$$

The motor boat can be hired for $2\frac{1}{2}$, 3, $3\frac{1}{2}$, 4, $4\frac{1}{2}$ or 5 hours.

(c)

EXERCISE   2

1   Use a number line to show the solutions to $4 < n \leqslant 7$ if n must be a whole number.

2   A printing firm prints leaflets at a standing charge of £20 plus £4 per pack of a hundred leaflets.

(a) Write down the inequality for the number of packs of leaflets, n, which can be printed for £50 or less.

(b) What is the largest number of packs which can be printed?

3   Assuming that n must be a positive whole number, find the solutions to these inequalities and show them on number lines.

(a) $3n - 2 < 11$

(b) $\frac{1}{2}n + 5 \leqslant 8$

(c) $3 < 2n - 5 < 13$

(d) $17 \leqslant 5n - 3 \leqslant 42$

4

Bulent and Rosun find that they have £60 in cash. Write down the inequality which shows how long they can hire a canal boat for. What is the longest possible time assuming that this must be a whole number of hours?

5   Karen, Kevin, Emma and Matthew wish to play tennis at the local club. They pay a fee for one day's membership and then a charge per hour for the court.

The inequality which describes the number of hours, t, for which they can play is $6t + 10 \leqslant 35$.

(a) What is the maximum amount they decide to spend?

(b) What is the membership fee?

(c) What is the charge per hour?

4.3 **Further inequalities**

Each of the inequalities in the last section had solutions which consisted of isolated points on the number line. Such inequalities are said to have **discrete** solutions.

In this section you will deal with inequalities which have **continuous** solutions.

E X A M P L E   2

$T = 15W + 20$ gives the time in minutes needed to cook a turkey weighing W kg. Write down and solve the inequality for the weights of turkey which can be cooked in 4 hours or less.

S O L U T I O N

4 hours is 240 minutes, so the inequality is $15W + 20 \leqslant 240$.

First solve $15W + 20 = 240$

$$15W = 220$$
$$W = 220 \div 15 = 14\tfrac{2}{3}\,\text{kg}$$

There is no reason why the turkey should weigh a whole number of kilograms, so any weight up to $14\tfrac{2}{3}$ kg is possible, and the solution is $W \leqslant 14\tfrac{2}{3}$.

This can be shown on a number line:

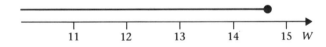

   TASKSHEET   1   —   Checking the sign (page 46)

When solving an inequality, you must first solve the equation which corresponds to the inequality and then decide which inequality sign you need in the answer.

The solution to $6 - 2x = 12$ is $x = {}^{-}3$.

Is $x < {}^{-}3$ or $x > {}^{-}3$ the solution to $6 - 2x < 12$?

EXERCISE 3

1 Explain carefully why the solution to the inequality $2x + 1 < 7$ is $x < 3$ and show the solution on a number line.

2 Jason said that the solution to $2x + 1 \leq 9$ was $x < 4$.

Explain where he went wrong.

3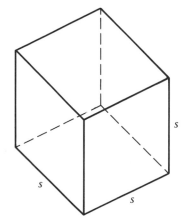

The inequality for the weight, W pounds, of a fruit cake you can cook in 2 hours or less is:

$$25W + 20 \leq 120$$

What are the missing numbers on the torn recipe leaflet?

4 Solve the inequalities:

(a) $2x - 1 \leq 23$ (b) $5(8 - x) \geq 20$

(c) $12 - 2x < 2$ (d) $\frac{1}{2}x - 4 > 5$

5 Write down **two** possible inequalities to fit each of the diagrams below.

(a)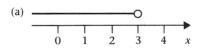

(b)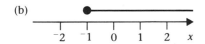

6 If a cube has each side of length s cm, the area of each face is s^2 cm².

Since the cube has 6 faces, the total area of paper needed to cover it is $6s^2$ cm².

So $6s^2 \leq 150$ describes the sizes of cubes which can be covered with 150 cm² of paper.

(a) Solve the inequality $6s^2 \leq 150$.

(b) Solve the inequality $6s^2 \leq 600$ and explain what the answer means.

7 Solve these inequalities, assuming that x is a positive number.

(a) $x^2 - 1 > 8$ (b) $x^2 + 11 \leq 47$ (c) $2x^2 \geq 32$

4.4 Inequalities and graphs

Joe's snacks

Hot dogs   50p
Hamburgers 60p

The number line shows the numbers of hot dogs that you can buy for £2 or less.

Draw a number line and show the numbers of Joe's hamburgers which you can buy for £2 or less.

In order to consider possible combinations of hot dogs and hamburgers which can be bought for various sums of money, you can use a graph rather than just a number line.

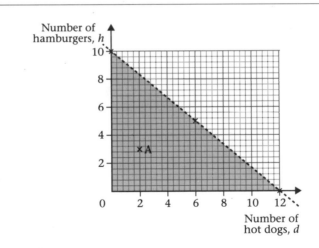

(a) Point A on the graph represents 2 hot dogs and 3 hamburgers. What is the cost of this combination?

(b) Write down the combinations given by the three points on the dotted line and work out the cost of each of them.

(c) What can you say about the costs of the combinations given by points below the dotted line?

(d) What is true about the costs of the combinations given by points above the line?

The dotted line on the graph on the previous page has equation:

$$50d + 60h = 600$$

The region underneath the line can be described as:

$$50d + 60h < 600$$

What is the inequality for the region above the line?

Any inequality involving **two variables** (two letters which can take different values) can be shown on a graph.

TASKSHEET 2 — *Graphing inequalities (page 47)*

After working through this chapter you should:

1 be able to write down and use formulas which describe practical situations;

2 be able to change the subject of a formula;

3 be able to solve an inequality like $2x - 3 < 7$ and show the solution on a number line;

4 understand that, since $x = 2$ is the solution to $11 - 3x = 5$, the solution to the inequality $11 - 3x \leqslant 5$ will be either $x \leqslant 2$ or $x \geqslant 2$, and know how to work out which it is;

5 be able to show inequalities like $y < 2x + 3$ on a graph.

Checking the sign

If	$17 - 4x = 5$
then	$12 - 4x = 0$
so	$4x = 12$
	$x = 3$

You might expect the solution of the inequality $17 - 4x > 5$ to be $x > 3$, but is this correct?

1 Copy and complete this table.

x	0	1	2	3	4	5	6
$17 - 4x$		13		5			

2 Your table should show that the solution of $17 - 4x > 5$ appears to be $x < 3$.

Check that this is also true when x is negative by working out the values of $17 - 4x$ when:

(a) $x = {}^-1$ (b) $x = {}^-3$

The solution of an inequality will always be linked to the solution of the corresponding equation, but you need to be careful about which symbol ($<$, $\leqslant$, $>$ or $\geqslant$) is needed. The following questions give you a method for doing this.

3 Work through the following steps to solve $3x - 7 > 8$.

(a) Check that the solution of $3x - 7 = 8$ is $x = 5$.

(b) Choose two or three values of x which are less than 5 and find the value of $3x - 7$ in each case. (0 is a good value to choose!)

(c) Does $x < 5$ seem to fit the inequality? If not, the solution should be $x > 5$.

(d) As a check, choose a value of x which is more than 5 and find the value of $3x - 7$.

4 Work though the following steps to solve $12 - \frac{1}{2}x < 7$.

(a) Solve the equation $12 - \frac{1}{2}x = 7$.

(b) Follow the method of question 3 parts (b), (c) and (d) to solve the inequality.

5 Solve the inequalities:

(a) $20 - 3x \leqslant 2$ (b) $2x - 7 \geqslant 9$

(c) $18 - \frac{1}{2}x < 10$ (d) $3(14 - x) > 18$

Graphing inequalities

1 (a) Write down the coordinates of any point on the line on the right.

   Check that the coordinates satisfy the equation $x + y = 6$.

   (b) Check that, for any point in region A, $x + y > 6$.

   (c) Check that, for any point in region B, $x + y < 6$.

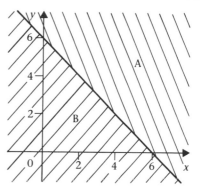

2

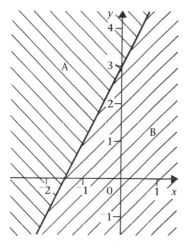

   (a) Explain why this line has equation $y = 2x + 3$.

   (b) Regions A and B could be labelled as $y > 2x + 3$ and $y < 2x + 3$.

   Which is which?

3 Write down the equation of the line opposite and use inequalities to describe the regions A and B.

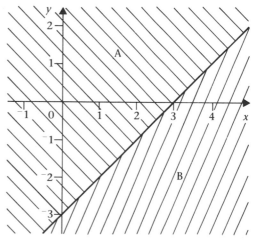

4 Draw a graph to show the region $y < 3x$.

5 Non-linear graphs

5.1 Parabolic and cubic graphs

Any graph which is not a straight line is said to be **non-linear**. Two examples of non-linear graphs which will be studied in this section are parabolic and cubic graphs.

The **parabola** is an interesting curve because you see it in many different situations. For example, if you look closely you will see that an object thrown through the air follows a path which is approximately parabolic.

 TASKSHEET 1 — Drawing graphs (page 58)

Although the parabolic curve keeps its basic shape, you can choose axes which make it look tall and narrow (like the path of a netball when you shoot for goal) or you can make it look short and fat (like the path of a netball when you do a pass). The word 'parabola' refers not just to one curve but to a whole family of curves.

The shape of the parabola is defined by the equation $y = x^2$.

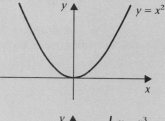

The graph of $y = x^3$ looks like this. It is called a **cubic** graph.

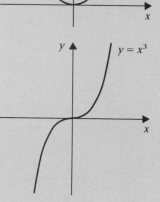

(a) Use a graph plotter on a computer or a graphic calculator to draw the following graphs. (Use the same axes with an x-range from $^-5$ to 5 and a y-range from 0 to 40.)

(i) $y = x^2$ (ii) $y = 5x^2$ (iii) $y = 0{\cdot}5x^2$

What do you notice? Describe the symmetry of the parabola. Can you explain why it has this symmetry?

(b) Use the graph plotter to draw the graph of $y = x^3$ (a cubic graph) with an x-range from $^-4$ to 4 and a y-range from $^-50$ to 50. Describe the symmetry of the cubic graph. Explain why it has this symmetry.

(c) Between which two positive whole numbers does x lie if:

(i) $x^2 = 20$;   (ii) $x^3 = 20$?

(d) How could you use your calculator to obtain more accurate answers to parts (i) and (ii) of question (c)?

5.2 **Trial and improvement**

The graph of an equation such as $y = 2x^2 - 5x$ will also give a parabolic curve.

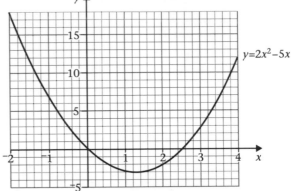

Plot the graph of $y = 2x^2 - 5x$ on a graph plotter and check that it looks like the graph shown above.

It is not too difficult to work out the value of y given a value of x.

E X A M P L E   1

If $y = 2x^2 - 5x$, find y when $x = 4$.

S O L U T I O N

$$y = 2 \times 4 \times 4 - 5 \times 4$$
$$= 32 - 20$$
$$= 12$$

It is more difficult to work out the value of x given a value of y.

E X A M P L E   2

Between which two positive whole numbers does x lie if $2x^2 - 5x = 10$?

S O L U T I O N

From the graph, $2x^2 - 5x$ is equal to 10 when x is just less than 4.

When $x = 3$, $2x^2 - 5x =$ 3.
When $x = 4$, $2x^2 - 5x = 12$.

This confirms that $3 < x < 4$.

You can get a more accurate solution to the equation $2x^2 - 5x = 10$ by trying different values of x between 3 and 4. This method is called **trial and improvement**.

EXAMPLE 3

Find the value of x (to 2 d.p.) so that $2x^2 - 5x = 10$ using the method of trial and improvement.

SOLUTION

x	$2x^2 - 5x$ (to 2 d.p.)	Comment
3	3	x is more than 3
4	12	x is less than 4
3·5	7	x is more than 3·5
3·9	10·92	x is less than 3·9
3·7	8·88	x is more than 3·7
3·8	9·88	x is more than 3·8
3·85	10·40	x is less than 3·85
3·82	10·08	x is less than 3·82
3·81	9·98	x is more than 3·81
3·815	10·03	x is less than 3·815

x is more than 3·81 but less than 3·815.

x is therefore 3·81 (to 2 d.p.).

EXERCISE 1

1 Round the following to the number of decimal places shown.

(a) 27·3729 (to 2 d.p.) (b) 0·0375 (to 3 d.p.)

(c) 30·999 99 (to 1 d.p.) (d) $3 \div 7$ (to 3 d.p.)

2 Use trial and improvement to find a positive value of x correct to 2 decimal places if $2x^2 + x - 25 = 0$. (Plot the graph on a computer using a graph plotting program and check your solution.)

3 Use trial and improvement to find x correct to 1 decimal place if $x^2 - 6x + 9 = 2$. (Use a graph plotter to check your solution.)

5.3 Direct proportion

Some things are said to increase or decrease in **direct proportion** to each other. For example the cost of buying bread is directly proportional to the number of loaves you buy. If you double the number of loaves, you double the cost, and if you halve the number of loaves you halve the cost. (This assumes the loaves are all the same size and type, and that there is no discount for bulk purchase!)

EXAMPLE 4

If 3 loaves cost £2·61, how much would 2 loaves cost?

SOLUTION

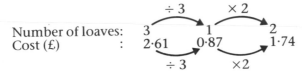

Number of loaves: 3   1   2
Cost (£)   :   2·61   0·87   1·74

3 loaves cost £2·61.

1 loaf costs £ $\dfrac{2 \cdot 61}{3}$ = £0·87.

2 loaves cost £0·87 × 2 = £1·74.

> If 7 buns cost £2·38, how much would 3 cost?

 TASKSHEET 2 – *Direct proportionality (page 59)*

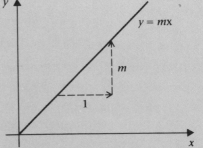

When two variables are in direct proportion, the graph is a straight line which passes through the origin.

The equation of the graph is $y = mx$.

m is called the **constant of proportionality**.

The symbol $\propto$ is often used to stand for 'is proportional to'.

If $y \propto x$ then $y = mx$.

To decide if two variables are in direct proportion, you can ask yourself the following question:

- Whenever I double one amount, does the other also double?

If your answer is 'yes' then the two variables are directly proportional.

EXERCISE 2

1 In which of the following data sets could y be directly proportional to x? In each case give a reason for your answer.

(a)

x	2	4	6	7
y	5	10	15	17·5

(b)

x	2	4	6	8
y	6	12	17	21

(c)

x	1	3	5	7
y	4	8	12	16

(d)

x	0	5
y	0	2

2 Which (if any) of the following graphs show $y \propto x$?

(a)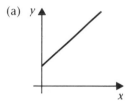

(b)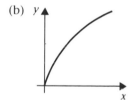

(c)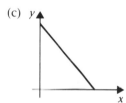

3 A plumber charges £15 per hour in addition to a call-out charge of £20.

(a) How much would he charge if you called him out to fix a burst pipe and the job took $2\frac{1}{2}$ hours?

(b) Is the amount he charges directly proportional to the time it takes to do the job? Explain your answer.

4 (a) Suppose a train travels at a speed of 60 m.p.h. Is the distance travelled directly proportional to the journey time?

(b) Find the time taken for the train to travel 120 miles at a speed of:

(i) 60 m.p.h.;   (ii) 40 m.p.h.;   (iii) 30 m.p.h.

(c) Is the time taken to complete a journey directly proportional to the speed of the train? Explain your answer.

5.4 Inverse proportion

Some things are said to increase or decrease in **inverse proportion** to each other. This means that as one amount increases, so the other decreases in the same proportion.

For example, the number of litres of petrol you can buy for £10 is inversely proportional to the cost of one litre. If, following an oil crisis, the price of petrol doubles then you can buy only half as much petrol with your £10.

E X A M P L E   5

You buy 7 litres of petrol at £0·50 per litre. Suppose the price of petrol goes up to £0·70 per litre. How many litres would you be able to buy for the same amount of money?

SOLUTION

Amount spent on petrol = 7 × £0·50 = £3·50

Suppose the amount of petrol bought at the new price is y litres.

$0·70 \times y = 3·50$ (The new price of petrol is £0·70 per litre.)

$$y = \frac{3·50}{0·70} = 5$$

You can buy 5 litres at the new price.

Note that the cost per litre goes up by the same proportion that the amount bought comes down.

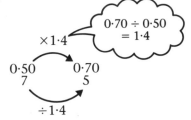

Cost per litre (£) :
Number of litres:

TASKSHEET 3 — Inverse proportionality (page 61)

When two variables, x and y, are inversely proportional, the graph looks like the one shown here.

The equation of the graph is:

$$xy = k \text{ or } y = \frac{k}{x}$$

where k is a constant number.

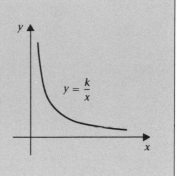

$y = \frac{k}{x}$

EXAMPLE 6

Does the following data set show that y is inversely proportional to x? Justify your answer.

x	2	4	6	8	16
y	24	12	8	6	3

SOLUTION

x and y appear to be inversely proportional because **all** the points fit the relationship $x \times y =$ a constant.

In this case $x \times y = 48$.

(a) (i) What does the graph of $xy = 48$ look like for negative values of x?

(ii) Sketch the graph for both positive and negative values of x.

(iii) Describe the symmetry of the graph.

(b) Use a graph plotter to draw the graph of $y = \frac{48}{x}$ and check your answer to (a) (i). (Use the same scale on both axes.)

(c) On the same axes draw the graphs of:

(i) $y = \frac{24}{x}$ (ii) $y = \frac{12}{x}$ (iii) $y = \frac{6}{x}$ (iv) $y = \frac{1}{x}$

When $k = 1$, you obtain the graph of $y = \dfrac{1}{x}$.

This is called the **reciprocal** graph

because $\dfrac{1}{x}$ is the **reciprocal** of x.

EXERCISE 3

1 If a job takes 9 days for 4 people to complete:

(a) how long would it take 6 people;

(b) how many people would be needed if the job had to be completed in 3 days? (Assume each person works at the same rate.)

2 Could y be inversely proportional to x for these data sets? Justify your answer.

(a)

x	2	6	12
y	30	10	5

(b)

x	1	2	6
y	26	13	4

3 Find a, given that y is inversely proportional to x in the following data sets.

(a)

x	3	15
y	10	a

(b)

x	1·4	3·5
y	5	a

(c)

x	2	a
y	12	6

(d)

x	10	15
y	a	3

4 A guitar player produces different notes from the same string by varying the length of the vibrating part of the string. The frequency, f, of the note (measured in hertz, Hz) is inversely proportional to the length, l, of the vibrating part of the string. The note whose frequency is 110 Hz is called A. If a string of length 70 cm has been tuned to produce this note, calculate the string length to produce the note called D which has a frequency 147 Hz.

After working through this chapter, you should:

1 be able to plot non-linear graphs;

2 be familiar with the following graphs:
- $y = x^2$,   a parabolic graph;
- $y = x^3$,   a cubic graph;
- $y = \dfrac{1}{x}$,   a reciprocal graph;

3 appreciate the symmetries of the parabolic and cubic graphs;

4 know how to use trial and improvement to solve non-linear equations;

5 know the meaning of direct and inverse proportionality.

Drawing graphs

1 (a) What is $^-2 \times {}^-2$?

   (b) If $y = x^2$ what is y when:

   (i) $x = {}^-2$ (ii) $x = 2$ (iii) $x = 3$ (iv) $x = {}^-3$

   (c) What is x when $y = 25$? (Is there more than one answer?)

2 Draw axes on a piece of graph paper with x from $^-5$ to 5 (using a scale of 1 cm to 2 units) and y from 0 to 25 (using a scale of 1 cm to 10 units). Now plot the (x, y) coordinates you calculated in 1(b). Calculate and plot some more points which fit the relationship $y = x^2$. Draw the graph of $y = x^2$. (Draw a smooth curve through the points.)

3 Redraw the graph using:

   (a) a scale of 1 cm to 1 unit on the x-axis (leaving the y-axis unchanged);

   (b) a scale of 1 cm to 2 units on both axes.

   Note that the same graph looks different depending on the scales you use.

4 (a) What is $^-2 \times {}^-2 \times {}^-2$?

   (b) If $y = x^3$, what is y when:

   (i) $x = {}^-2$ (ii) $x = 2$ (iii) $x = 1 \cdot 5$ (iv) $x = {}^-1 \cdot 5$

   (c) What is x when $y = 27$? (Is there more than one answer?)

5 Draw axes on a piece of graph paper with x from $^-3$ to 3 (using a scale of 2 cm to 1 unit) and with y from $^-30$ to 30 (using a scale of 1 cm to 5 units). Now plot the (x, y) coordinates you calculated in 4(b). Calculate and plot some more points which fit the relationship $y = x^3$. Draw the graph of $y = x^3$.

Direct proportionality

Lisbeth has cornflakes with milk for breakfast. She reads on the packet that a typical serving consists of 30 grams of cereal and that this provides her with 120 calories (a measure of energy content).

1 The packet of cornflakes contains 600 grams.

    (a) How many typical servings are there in a packet?

    (b) How many calories are there in a packet?

You can think of question 1 in the following way:

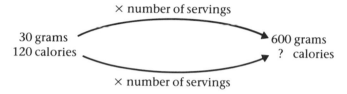

The number of calories is directly proportional to the number of grams.

If, for example, you double or treble the number of grams then you will also double or treble the number of calories.

2 Lisbeth does not always have a typical serving. She may have more or less according to how hungry she feels.

    (a) Copy and complete the following table.

Grams of cereal, x	10	20	30	40	50	60
Number of calories, y			120			

    (b) Draw x- and y-axes on graph paper using a scale which allows you to plot all the points in the table. Plot the points and draw the graph.

    (c) How many calories are there in 1 gram of cereal?

    (d) For each of the points in the table, calculate $y \div x$. What do you notice?

    (e) Write down the equation of your graph.

    (f) Check your answer to (e) by plotting your points on a graph plotter and superimposing the graph of your equation.

3 500 ml (half a litre) of milk provide 300 calories.

(a) How many calories does Lisbeth get for breakfast if she has 25 grams of cornflakes and 125 ml of milk?

(b) Copy and complete the following table.

Volume of milk (ml), x	50	100	200	500	1000
Number of calories, y				300	

(c) Draw x- and y-axes on graph paper using a scale which allows you to plot all the points in the table. Plot the points and draw the graph.

(d) How many calories are there in 1 ml of milk?

(e) For each of the points in the table, calculate $y \div x$. What do you notice?

(f) Write down the equation of your graph.

(g) Check your answer to (e) by plotting your points on a graph plotter and superimposing the graph of your equation.

4 Iron is one of many trace elements needed for good health. (A lack of iron in your diet will eventually result in anaemia.) The recommended daily intake of iron for an adult is 12 milligrams (mg). A 25 gram serving of cereal will provide you with approximately 2 mg of iron.

(a) Copy and complete the following table.

Grams of cereal, x	1	5	10	25	100
Milligrams of iron, y				2	

(b) What is the gradient of the graph?

(c) Use your answer to (b) to write down the equation of the graph.

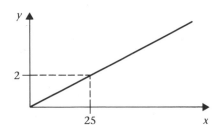

Inverse proportionality

1 The distance from the village of Thurston to Cambridge is 32 miles.

(a) How long would it take to travel from Thurston to Cambridge if your average speed was 8 m.p.h.?

(b) If you double your average speed, do you double the time it takes to complete the journey?

(c) In this case is speed directly proportional to time?

(d) Copy and complete the following table.

Average speed, x m.p.h.	1	2	4	8	16	32
Journey time, y hours						

(e) Draw x- and y-axes on a piece of graph paper using a scale such that all the (x, y) points in the table completed in (d) can be plotted. Plot the points and draw the graph.

(f) What do you get if you multiply the x-coordinate by the y-coordinate for each of the points in your table?

2 You have £1·20 to spend on sweets.

(a) How many grams will you get if you spend all your money on sweets which cost 20p for 50 grams?

(b) Copy and complete the following table.

Cost per 50 grams, x pence	5	10	20	30	40	60
Amount you can buy, y grams		600				

(c) Draw x- and y-axes on a piece of graph paper using a scale such that all the (x, y) points in the table completed in (b) can be plotted. Plot the points and draw the graph.

(d) What do you get if you multiply the x-coordinate by the y-coordinate for each of the points in your table?

(e) If you double x, what happens to y?

6 Brackets and indices

6.1 Using brackets

The framework of this box-kite needs 4 pieces of wood of length a cm, 4 pieces of length b cm and 4 pieces of length c cm.

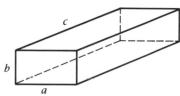

(a) What is the total length of wood needed if $a = 15$, $b = 12$ and $c = 8$ cm?

(b) Explain why the total length needed (L cm) can be given by both $L = 4a + 4b + 4c$ and $L = 4(a + b + c)$.

(c) The shaded area is given approximately by:

$$A = 3R^2 - 3r^2$$

What is the area if $r = 4$ cm and $R = 5$ cm?

(d) Check that you get the same answer to (c) by using the formula:

$$A = 3(R^2 - r^2)$$

(e) By choosing any values for a, b and c, show that:

$$3(a + 2b + 5c) = 3a + 6b + 15c$$

EXAMPLE 1

Write $3(2x + 4y)$ as $(2x + 4y) + (2x + 4y) + (2x + 4y)$ and hence show that $3(2x + 4y) = 6x + 12y$.

SOLUTION

$$3(2x + 4y) = 2x + 4y + 2x + 4y + 2x + 4y \qquad ①$$
$$= 2x + 2x + 2x + 4y + 4y + 4y \qquad ②$$
$$= 6x + 12y \qquad ③$$

Going from line ① to line ② is possible because the order in which numbers are added does not matter. For example,

$$3 + 5 + 7 = 5 + 3 + 7 = 3 + 7 + 5$$

Going from line ② to line ③ is simply a matter of adding all the terms with x and all the terms with y.

The whole process of going from line ① to line ③ is one of **simplifying the expression** by collecting together **like terms**.

An algebraic expression can be simplified by collecting together terms which are like each other.

- Terms such as ^+3a, ^+5a and ^-2a are **like** terms.

- Terms such as ^+3a, ^+3ab and $^-3a^2$ are **unlike** terms.

EXERCISE 1

1 (a) Write down an expression for the total length of wood needed for this kite:

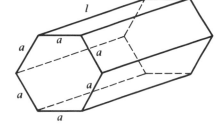

   (i) using brackets;

   (ii) without brackets.

   (b) Show that both expressions give the same answer for the length of wood when $a = 12$ cm and $l = 30$ cm.

2 Write each of these expressions without brackets.

   (a) $2(3x + 4y)$ (b) $2(3a + 2b + 4c)$ (c) $3(4 + 2c + 3a)$

3 $3(x + 4y) + 4(y + 2x) = 3x + 12y + 4y + 8x = 11x + 16y$

Use this method to write the following expressions as simply as possible.

(a) $2(a + 4c) + 3(2a + c)$

(b) $3(2x + 3y) + 2(x + 2y)$

4

A hollow rubber ball has inner radius r and outer radius R.

Since the volume of a sphere is given by:

$$V = \tfrac{4}{3}\pi r^3$$

the volume of rubber is given by:

$$V = \tfrac{4}{3}\pi R^3 - \tfrac{4}{3}\pi r^3$$

(a) Using brackets, write the expression for the volume of rubber.

(b) What is this volume when $R = 10\,$cm and $r = 9{\cdot}5\,$cm?

5 Copy and complete this solution of the equation:

$$4(x - 6) = x + 3$$
$$4x - 24 = x + 3 \qquad \text{(Multiply out the bracket.)}$$
$$3x - 24 = 3 \qquad \text{(Take } x \text{ from both sides.)}$$

6 Solve the equations:

(a) $3(2x + 1) = 4x + 5$

(b) $7x - 4 = 2(x + 8)$

(c) $3(x + 2) = 2x - 5$

(d) $4(2x - 3) = 3(x + 7)$

7 (a) Explain why $a \times 3a$ can be written as $3a^2$ and why $a \times 2b = 2ab$. Hence explain why:

$$a(3a + 2b) = 3a^2 + 2ab$$

(b) Write without brackets:

(i) $c(c + d)$

(ii) $c(2c + 3d)$

(iii) $2x(x - 3y)$

(iv) $d(3c - 2d)$

6.2 Formulas and brackets

When changing the subject of a formula which includes brackets, it is not always necessary to multiply out the brackets.

EXAMPLE 2

The end of this box-kite is a rectangle with dimensions j and k.

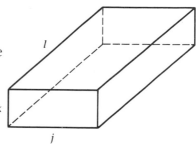

The length of the kite is l.

The total length of wood needed to make the frame is $T = 4(j + k + l)$.

(a) Rearrange the formula to give the length, l, of the kite in terms of T, j and k.

(b) How long can the kite be if $j = 8\,$cm, $k = 10\,$cm and the total length of wood available is $136\,$cm?

SOLUTION

(a) The formula needs to be rearranged to make l the subject. It is probably easiest to use balance diagrams.

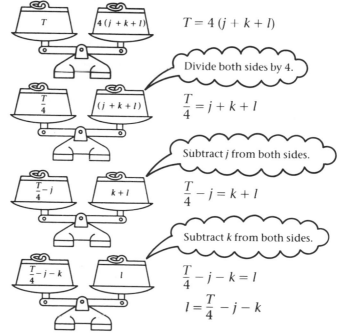

$T = 4(j + k + l)$

Divide both sides by 4.

$\dfrac{T}{4} = j + k + l$

Subtract j from both sides.

$\dfrac{T}{4} - j = k + l$

Subtract k from both sides.

$\dfrac{T}{4} - j - k = l$

$l = \dfrac{T}{4} - j - k$

(b) $l = (136 \div 4) - 8 - 10 = 16\,$cm

65

EXERCISE 2

1 A kite is to be made shaped like an octagonal prism.

The ends are regular octagons with each side of length p cm.

The length of the kite is l cm.

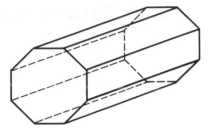

(a) Explain why the length of wood needed for the frame is given by:

$$T = 16p + 8l$$

(b) Rearrange the formula to make l the subject.

(c) How long can the kite be if $p = 7$ cm and the total length of wood to be used is 240 cm?

2 Copy and complete this method for making b the subject of the formula $A = \frac{1}{2}h(a + b)$.

$$A = \tfrac{1}{2}h(a + b)$$

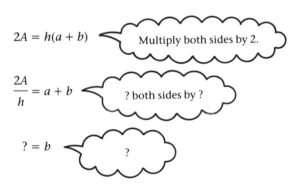

$$2A = h(a + b)$$ Multiply both sides by 2.

$$\frac{2A}{h} = a + b$$? both sides by ?

$$? = b$$?

3 Make x the subject of each of these formulas.

(a) $h = 3(x + b)$ (b) $y = \frac{1}{2}(3x - 2)$

4 (a) Make x the subject of the formula $y = 4(x + 3b)$.

(b) Make b the subject of the formula $y = 4(x + 3b)$.

6.3 Index form

You are already familiar with the terms **squared** and **cubed**.

Write 4 down twice and multiply.

Four squared $4^2 = 4 \times 4 = 16$

Two cubed $2^3 = 2 \times 2 \times 2 = 8$

Write 2 down three times and multiply.

In the same way: $3^4 = 3 \times 3 \times 3 \times 3$

(a) What is the value of 3^4?

(b) Work out the value of 4^5. (The answer is **not** 20!)

4^5 is in index form.
It is written in words as
'4 to the power of 5'.
The 4 is the **base** and the
5 is the **power** or **index**.

base

4^5

index
number
or power

(a) Write down, in index form, 6 to the power of 3.

(b) 'The base is 2 and the index number 5.' Write down the
value of the number being described.

A scientific calculator has a key to enable you to evaluate a power of

a number. The key looks like $\boxed{x^y}$ or $\boxed{y^x}$.

(a) Find this key on your calculator.

If you key in $\boxed{2}$ $\boxed{x^y}$ $\boxed{3}$ the calculator will evaluate 2^3.
Do this and check that you get the answer 8.

(b) Use your calculator to evaluate:

(i) 4^6 (ii) 6^4 (iii) 2^8

EXAMPLE 3

Evaluate $3^5 \times 6^3$.

SOLUTION

Your calculator will automatically work out powers before other arithmetical operations, so you just need to key in:

$$\boxed{3}\;\boxed{x^y}\;\boxed{5}\;\boxed{\times}\;\boxed{6}\;\boxed{x^y}\;\boxed{3}$$

This gives the answer 52 488.

If in doubt, you can always use brackets and key in:

$$\boxed{(}\;\boxed{3}\;\boxed{x^y}\;\boxed{5}\;\boxed{)}\;\boxed{\times}\;\boxed{(}\;\boxed{6}\;\boxed{x^y}\;\boxed{3}\;\boxed{)}$$

EXERCISE 3

1 Use your calculator to evaluate:

(a) 4^6 (b) 8^5 (c) 9^4 (d) 11^6

2 Work out:

(a) (i) 3^5 (ii) $3^2 \times 3^3$

(b) (i) 2^6 (ii) $2^2 \times 2^4$ (iii) $2^3 \times 2^3$

(c) (i) 4^7 (ii) $4^3 \times 4^4$ (iii) $4^5 \times 4^2$ (iv) $4^2 \times 4^2 \times 4^3$

3 Look carefully at your answers to question 2 and describe a quick way of working out c if you are told that $3^3 \times 3^5 = 3^c$.

4 Ann said that it was obvious that $6^7 \div 6^3 = 6^4$.

(a) Why did she say this?

(b) Check with your calculator that she was right.

5 (a) $(a^4)^3 = a^4 \times a^4 \times a^4$. Explain why $a^4 \times a^4 \times a^4 = a^{12}$.

(b) Write as simply as possible:

(i) $(a^4)^2$ (ii) $(b^4)^4$ (iii) $(x^3)^5$

(c) Describe a quick method for writing $(a^5)^6$ more simply.

6.4 **Rules of indices**

Exercise 3 demonstrated the **rules of indices**. (Indices is the plural of index.)

These rules can be written as:

For any numbers x, a and b:

- $x^a \times x^b = x^{a+b}$
- $x^a \div x^b = x^{a-b}$
- $(x^a)^b = x^{ab}$

EXERCISE 4

1 Write down, as powers of p, the answers to:

(a) $p^3 \times p^5$ (b) $(p^6)^2$

(c) $p^2 \times p^3 \times p^5$ (d) $p^7 \div p^4$

(e) $p^4 \times p^2 \div p^3$ (f) $(p^2 \times p^4 \div p^3) \times p^2$

2 Using the laws of indices, $3^4 \times 3^5$ can be written as 3^9. Where possible, simplify the expressions using the laws of indices. Where it is not possible, explain why not.

(a) $3^4 \times 3^6$ (b) $3^4 \times 4^2$ (c) $(3^5)^3$

(d) $7^4 \div 6^3$ (e) $4^6 \times 3^4$ (f) $2^7 \div 2^3$

3 a^2b^3 means $a^2 \times b^3$.

Work out the value of a^2b^3 when $a = 4$ and $b = 5$.

4 (a) Explain why $cddcg$ can be written as c^2d^2g.

(b) Write as simply as possible:

(i) xax (ii) $acacbb$ (iii) $xbbaba$

6.5 Factorising and indices

It is sometimes helpful to put brackets **into** an expression. This process is called **factorising** the expression.

TASKSHEET 1 — Factorising (page 73)

The tasksheet gave you practice in factorising expressions like $3a + 6b - 9c$ by spotting the common factor of the expression.

At times, particularly if the expression involves indices, spotting the common factor is more difficult.

> Explain why $x^2y + 3ax = x(xy + 3a)$.

E X A M P L E 3

Factorise $x^2y + 3xy$.

S O L U T I O N

The expression has two terms, x^2y and $3xy$.

x^2y means $x \times x \times y$ and $3xy$ means $3 \times x \times y$.

x and y are factors of both terms, so xy is a common factor of the expression.

So $x^2y + 3xy = xy(x + 3)$.

> Factorise each of these expressions.
>
> (a) $p^2q - 3pq$ (b) $p^2q + pq^2$ (c) $abc - bcd$
>
> (d) $a^2x + abx$ (e) $2x^2y + 6xy$ (f) $a^2bc + ab^2c$

6.6 More brackets

If you have a rectangle whose width is $a + b$ and whose length is $c + d$, its area would be $(a + b) \times (c + d)$. The diagram shows how this area can be split into 4 smaller regions.

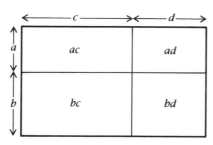

The area of the whole rectangle is:

$(a + b)(c + d)$

The four smaller regions are labelled with their areas. Make sure that you can see why:

$(a + b)(c + d) = ac + ad + bc + bd$

The area diagram can be replaced by a multiplication table.

×	c	d
a	ac	ad
b	bc	bd

So $(a + b)(c + d) = ac + ad + bc + bd$

From the table opposite, explain why:

$(3x + 2)(4x + 3) = 12x^2 + 9x + 8x + 6$

$\qquad\qquad\qquad\quad = 12x^2 + 17x + 6$

×	4x	3
3x	12x²	?
2	?	?

To multiply out two brackets where one or other of the brackets contains a subtraction sign, you need to know that:

$$a \times {}^-a = {}^-a^2 \quad \text{and} \quad {}^-a \times {}^-a = a^2$$

Write down simpler expressions for:

(a) $^-2x \times x$ (b) $^-3d \times {}^-2d$ (c) $3 \times {}^-2g$

(d) $^-3 \times 4y$ (e) $2c \times {}^+5d$ (f) $^-5x \times {}^-3$

EXAMPLE 4

Multiply out $(3x - 4)(2x + 3)$.

SOLUTION

You can use the multiplication table to multiply out $(3x - 4)(2x + 3)$ if you think of $(3x - 4)$ as $(3x + {}^-4)$.

$\times$	$2x$	3
$3x$	$6x^2$	$9x$
$^-4$	^-8x	$^-12$

$$(3x - 4)(2x + 3) = 3x\,(2x + 3) - 4(2x + 3)$$
$$= 6x^2 + 9x - 8x - 12$$
$$= 6x^2 + x - 12$$

EXERCISE 5

1 For each of these expressions, draw a multiplication table to help you to multiply out the brackets, then write your answer as simply as possible.

(a) $(x + 2)(x + 3)$ (b) $(2x + 3)(3x + 4)$ (c) $(2a + 3)(a + 6)$

2 Write these expressions without brackets and as simply as possible. You may be able to do these without drawing a table.

(a) $(3a + 1)(a + 5)$ (b) $(2n + 5)(3n + 2)$ (c) $(4x + 2)(2x + 3)$

3 Multiply out:

(a) $(3x - 4)(x + 3)$ (b) $(2x + 5)(3x - 2)$

4 Use a multiplication table to help explain why:

$$(2x - 3)(3x - 4) = 6x^2 - 9x - 8x + 12 = 6x^2 - 17x + 12$$

5 Multiply out:

(a) $(3x - 4)(x - 3)$ (b) $(2x - 5)(3x - 2)$

After working through this chapter, you should:

1 know how to multiply out brackets, for example:

$$(x + 1)^2 = (x + 1)(x + 1) = x^2 + 2x + 1$$

2 know how to factorise an expression, for example:

$$a^2 + 2ab = a(a + 2b)$$

3 know how to evaluate numbers expressed in index form.

Factorising

1 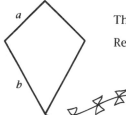 The distance round the outside of this kite is $2a + 2b$.

Rewrite this expression for the distance, using brackets.

2 The total length of the framework for this octagonal prism kite is given by:

$$T = 16a + 8b$$

Explain why it could also be

$$T = 8(2a + b)$$

Both $16a$ and $8b$ can be divided by 8, so 8 is called the **common factor** of $16a$ and $8b$.

3 Copy and complete the following expressions.

(a) $3c + 6d = 3(c + \quad)$ (b) $12a + 16b = 4(\qquad)$

(c) $9x - 12y = 3(\quad - \quad)$ (d) $4x - 14y = 2(\qquad)$

4 (a) Write down the common factors of:

    (i) $8c$ and $4d$ (ii) $6c$ and $18b$

    (iii) $14x$ and $10y$ (iv) $9y$ and $21x$

(b) Use your answers to (a) to write these expressions using brackets.

    (i) $8c + 4d$ (ii) $6c + 18b$

    (iii) $14x - 10y$ (iv) $9y - 21x$

5 (a) Explain why $12x + 18y = 2(6x + 9y)$.

(b) Try to find another way of factorising $12x + 18y$.

6 Rewrite the following expressions using brackets.

(a) $3a + 6b - 9c$ (b) $8x + 4y - 12z$

(c) $7d + 14e - 21f$ (d) $12b + 6c + 15d$

Solutions

1 Straight-line graphs

1.1 Story graphs

Imagine you are on the ride. Sketch a graph which shows how your speed changes with time as you go from A to D.

Do not worry about values on the axes for speed and time. Simply draw a graph which shows how you think the speed changes.

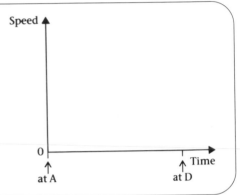

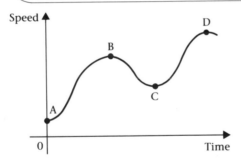

1.2 Linear graphs

You can plot a linear graph if you know at least two points. Why is it advisable to plot at least three points?

Any two points can be joined by a straight line, so if you make a mistake it will not be obvious that an error has occurred. Three points cannot be joined by a straight line unless they all fit the equation of the line. It is therefore sensible to work out three points for a given equation.

EXERCISE 1

1 (a) (i) $y = 2$ (ii) $y = 5$ (iii) $y = 0$

(b) The straight line should go through $(0, 0)$, $(4, 2)$ and $(10, 5)$.

2 (a) and (b)

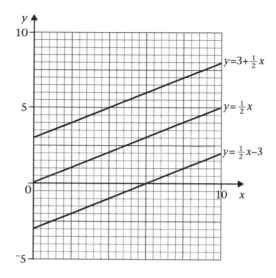

(c) The three graphs are parallel straight lines.

1.3 Gradient

(a) Describe a line which has zero gradient.

(b) Does a vertical line have a gradient?

(a) Horizontal lines have zero gradient – the obvious example is the x-axis.

(b) For a vertical line, the horizontal change will be zero, so the gradient will be:

$$\frac{y \text{ change}}{0}$$

It is impossible to divide by 0 so the gradient cannot be given a number.

E X E R C I S E 2

1 (a) and (b) have positive gradients.

(c) and (d) have negative gradients.

2 (a) The gradient is $\dfrac{(10 - 7)}{(5 - 2)} = \dfrac{3}{3} = 1.$

(b) The gradient is $\dfrac{(5 - 7)}{(6 - 2)} = \dfrac{^-2}{4} = ^-0\cdot5.$

(c) The gradient is $\dfrac{(10 - 1)}{(^-2 - 4)} = \dfrac{9}{^-6} = ^-1\cdot5.$

(d) The gradient is $\dfrac{(5-5)}{(4-\,^{-}1)} = \dfrac{0}{5} = 0.$

(e) The gradient is $\dfrac{(7\cdot2-3\cdot6)}{(3\cdot7-1\cdot2)} = \dfrac{3\cdot6}{2\cdot5} = 1\cdot44.$

(f) The gradient is $\dfrac{(5\cdot7-3\cdot0)}{(0\cdot5-\,^{-}2\cdot3)} = \dfrac{2\cdot7}{2\cdot8} = 0\cdot96$ (to 2 d.p.).

2 Graphs and equations

2.2 Solving equations

Write down and solve the equation to determine for how long you can hire a boat for £14.

The equation is $\qquad\qquad 2h + 4 = 14.$
Taking 4 from both sides: $\qquad 2h = 10$
Halving both sides: $\qquad\qquad h = 5$
The boat can be hired for 5 hours.

Check that $5x - 7$ does in fact equal $2x + 8$ when $x = 5$.

If $x = 5$, $5x - 7 = 25 - 7 = 18$
If $x = 5$, $2x + 8 = 10 + 8 = 18$

EXERCISE 1

1   (a) $3x + 7 = 34$
$\qquad\quad 3x = 27$
$\qquad\quad\; x = \;\, 9$

(b) $17 = 2x - 3$
$\qquad 20 = 2x$
$\qquad 10 = x$

(c) $\tfrac{1}{3}x + 5 = 15$
$\qquad \tfrac{1}{3}x = 10$
$\qquad\; x = 30$

(d) $5x + 1\cdot4 = 7\cdot6$
$\qquad\; 5x = 6\cdot2$
$\qquad\quad x = 1\cdot24$

2 (a) $3x + 5x - 2x = 8x - 2x = 6x$

   (b) $4x + 17 - x + 3 = 4x - x + 17 + 3 = 3x + 20$

3 (a) $7x - 5 = 3x + 27$

   $\quad\quad 4x - 5 = 27 \quad\quad$ (Take $3x$ from both sides.)

   $\quad\quad\quad 4x = 32 \quad\quad$ (Add 5 to both sides.)

   $\quad\quad\quad\; x = 8 \quad\quad$ (Divide both sides by 4.)

   (b) $\;x + 5 = 41 - 3x$

   $\quad\quad 4x + 5 = 41 \quad\quad$ (Add $3x$ to both sides.)

   $\quad\quad\quad 4x = 36 \quad\quad$ (Subtract 5 from both sides.)

   $\quad\quad\quad\; x = 9 \quad\quad$ (Divide both sides by 4.)

2.3 The point of intersection

> Draw the graphs of $y = 4 + 2x$ and $y = 24 - 3x$ on graph paper (or use a graph plotter) and check that they intersect at the point (4, 12).

If both graphs do not pass through the point (4, 12) you have made a mistake!

E X E R C I S E 2

1 (a) $4x - 12 = x + 3$

   $\quad\quad 3x - 12 = 3$

   $\quad\quad\quad 3x = 15$

   $\quad\quad\quad\; x = 5$

   $\quad\quad y = 4 \times 5 - 12 = 8 \quad$ (or $\;y = 5 + 3 = 8$)

   (b) $2x - 1 = x - 8$

   $\quad\quad x - 1 = {}^-8$

   $\quad\quad\quad x = {}^-7$

   $\quad\quad y = 2 \times {}^-7 - 1 = {}^-15 \quad$ (or $\;y = {}^-7 - 8 = {}^-15$)

   (c) $\frac{1}{2}x + 2 = 11 - x$

   $\quad\quad 1\frac{1}{2}x + 2 = 11$

   $\quad\quad\quad 1\frac{1}{2}x = 9$

   $\quad\quad\quad\; x = 6$

   $\quad\quad y = \frac{1}{2} \times 6 + 2 = 5 \quad$ (or $\;y = 11 - 6 = 5$)

2 At corner A, the lines $y = 5x - 15$ and $y = 45 - x$ meet where:

   $\quad 5x - 15 = 45 - x$

   $\quad 6x - 15 = 45$

   $\quad\quad 6x = 60$

   $\quad\quad\; x = 10 \quad$ and $\quad y = 35$

At corner B, the lines $y = 5x - 15$ and $y = 9 + 0{\cdot}2x$ meet where:

$5x - 15 = 9 + 0{\cdot}2x$
$4{\cdot}8x - 15 = 9$
$\quad 4{\cdot}8x = 24$
$\qquad x = 5 \quad$ and $\quad y = 10$

At corner C, the lines $y = 45 - x$ and $y = 9 + 0{\cdot}2x$ meet where:

$45 - x = 9 + 0{\cdot}2x$
$\quad 45 = 9 + 1{\cdot}2x$
$\quad 36 = 1{\cdot}2x$
$\quad\ x = 30 \quad$ and $\quad y = 15$

The corners of the triangle are A(10, 35), B(5, 10), C(30, 15).

2.4   Simultaneous equations

Explain why $3x + 4y = 400$.

3 small cones cost $x + x + x = 3x$ pence.
4 large cones cost $y + y + y + y = 4y$ pence.
The total cost is 400 pence and so:

$$3x + 4y = 400$$

E X E R C I S E   3

1   (a) $2x + y = 31$
$\quad\ \ x + y = 17$

$\quad x \qquad\ = 14 \quad$ so $14 + y = 17$ and $y = 3$

(b) The graphs will intersect at (14, 3).

(c) $x + y = 17$ can be rewritten as $y = 17 - x$.
$2x + y = 31$ can be rewritten as $y = 31 - 2x$.

The point (14, 3) is therefore on both lines and so must be the point at which the lines intersect.

2   (a) $4x + 2y = 10$
$\quad\ \ x + 2y =\ \ 7$

$\quad 3x \qquad\ = 3$

$\qquad x =\ \ 1 \quad$ so $4 + 2y = 10$ and $y = 3$
$\quad$(Check that $x = 1$ and $y = 3$ fit $x + 2y = 7$.)

(b) $3x + 2y = 15$
     $3x + y = 12$

     $\underline{y = 3}$ so $3x + 6 = 15$ and $x = 3$

(Check that $x = 3$ and $y = 3$ also fit $3x + y = 12$.)

3   (a) 2 hot dogs and 3 hamburgers cost 255p. ①
         1 hot dog and 4 hamburgers cost 265p. ②
         2 hot dogs and 8 hamburgers cost 530p. ③   (Multiply ② by 2.)
         5 hamburgers cost $530 - 255 = 275$p.   ③ $-$ ①
         So 1 hamburger costs 55p.
         1 hot dog costs $265 - 4 \times 55 = 45$p.
         A hot dog costs 45p and a hamburger costs 55p.

   (b) 2 hot dogs and 1 hamburger cost £1.45, not £1.55.

4   (a) $2x + y = 15$ so $4x + 2y = 30$ (Multiply by 2.)
                            $3x + 2y = 24$

         $\underline{x = 6}$ so $12 + y = 15$ and $y = 3$

(Check that $x = 6$ and $y = 3$ also fit $3x + 2y = 24$.)

   (b) $3x + 5y = 31$ so $6x + 10y = 62$ (Multiply by 2.)
         $2x + 3y = 20$ so $6x + 9y = 60$ (Multiply by 3.)

         $\underline{y = 2}$ so $3x + 10 = 31$ and $x = 7$

(Check that $x = 7$ and $y = 2$ also fit $2x + 3y = 20$.)

3 Sequences

3.1 Number patterns

> (a) What are the next two terms in the sequence
>
> $4, 7, 10, 13, \ldots$?
>
> (b) Describe carefully what pattern allows you to continue listing the
>   sequence.

(a) 16, 19

(b) Each term is formed by adding 3 to the previous term.

(a) Write down a number sequence for each of the spatial arrangements below.

(i) • •• ••• ••••
       •• ••• ••••
          ••• ••••
             ••••

(ii) •
     • ••
   • •• •••
• •• ••• ••••

(b) Describe the spatial arrangements and explain how you can continue the number sequences.

(a) (i) 1, 4, 9, 16, ...   (ii) 1, 3, 6, 10, ...

(b) (i) This is a pattern of squares. The next numbers will be $5^2 = 25$, then $6^2 = 36$ and so on. These numbers are called **square numbers**.

(ii) This is a pattern of triangles. The difference between one term and the next increases by one as the sequence progresses. The next two terms, for example, can be found as shown.

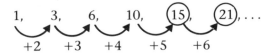

$$1, \quad 3, \quad 6, \quad 10, \quad 15, \quad 21, \, ...$$
$$\quad +2 \quad +3 \quad +4 \quad +5 \quad +6$$

These numbers are called **triangle numbers.**

EXERCISE 1

1 (a) 13, 10   The tenth term is 1.   (b) 25, 36   The tenth term is 100.

(c) 19, 23   The tenth term is 39.   (d) 21, 28   The tenth term is 55.

(e) $\frac{5}{6}, \frac{6}{7}$ The tenth term is $\frac{10}{11}$.

2 There are several possible arrangements for each. For example:

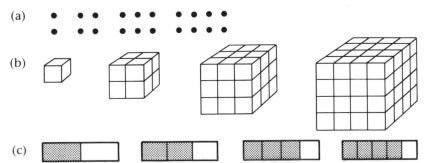

(a) • •• ••• ••••
     • •• ••• ••••

(b)

(c)

3.2 Further sequences

(a) What are the next two terms in the sequence? (In other words, what will be the next bid by the trader and the next offer from the customer?)

(b) What difference would it make if the customer started the bidding? (Write down the first six terms of the sequence.)

(a) 3500, 3250

(b) The sequence would be:

2000, 6000, 4000, 5000, 4500, 4750, . . .

You can see that this is of advantage to the trader.

E X E R C I S E   2

1 (a) $\frac{8}{21}, \frac{13}{34}$ (b) $7\frac{1}{2}, 7\frac{1}{4}$ (c) 16, 26

2 (a)

	Trader	Customer
Bid (drachmas)	4000	2000
	3000	2500
	2750	2625
	2687·50	

(b)

	Customer	Trader
Bid (drachmas)	2000	4000
	3000	3500
	3250	3375
	3312·50	

The trader should bid second to ensure that the highest possible price is eventually agreed on.

3.3 The general term

Explain why this shows that the rth term is $3r + 1$.

Each arrangement of r squares can be pictured as r sets of three matches, plus one at the end.

So ▢▢▢▢ ... ▢ becomes ⊏ ⊏ ⊏ ⊏ ... ⊏ ▮

$$3 \quad +3 \quad +3 \quad +3+ \ldots +3 \quad +1$$
$$\text{or} \quad 3r+1$$

> Relate this sequence to the square numbers and find an expression for the general term.
>
> $2, 5, 10, 17, 26, \ldots$

Square numbers	1	4	9	16	25	...	r^2	...
Sequence	2	5	10	17	26	...	$r^2 + 1$	...

EXERCISE 3

1 (a) 1, 3, 5, 7, 9   (b) 1, 8, 27, 64, 125

   (c) 1, 7, 17, 31, 49   (d) $0, \frac{1}{3}, \frac{2}{4}, \frac{3}{5}, \frac{4}{6}$

2 (a) $\dfrac{r(r+1)}{2} + 1$ (triangle numbers + 1)   (b) $r(r+1)$

3 (a) $2r$ (b) $2r+1$ (c) $6r-1$ (d) $\dfrac{r}{r+1}$

4 Formulas and inequalities

4.1 Formulas

> The conversion formula, $F = 1\cdot8C + 32$, can be used to change between °F and °C.
>
> For the biscuits, $F = 300$, so $300 = 1\cdot8C + 32$.
> At what temperature, in °C, should Paul have set his oven?

$$1\cdot8C = 300 - 32 = 268$$
$$C = \frac{268}{1\cdot8} = 149°, \text{ to the nearest degree}$$

Use balance diagrams to make x the subject of $y = \dfrac{x+5}{4}$.

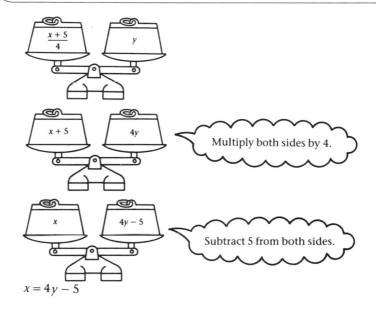

Multiply both sides by 4.

Subtract 5 from both sides.

$$x = 4y - 5$$

E X E R C I S E   1

1　(a)　$2 \times 40 + 30 = 110$ minutes or 1 hour 50 minutes

　　(b)　
$$T = 40W + 30$$
$$T - 30 = 40W \qquad \text{(Subtract 30 from both sides.)}$$
$$\frac{T - 30}{40} = W \quad \text{or} \quad W = \frac{T - 30}{40} \qquad \text{(Divide both sides by 40.)}$$

　　(c)　3 hours 10 minutes = 190 minutes
$$\text{so } W = \frac{(190 - 30)}{40} = 4$$
　　A 4 kg piece of meat can be cooked in 3 hours 10 minutes.

2　(a)　
$$u = 7a - 6$$
$$u + 6 = 7a$$
$$a = \frac{u + 6}{7}$$

　　(b)　
$$V = \frac{a - 5}{2}$$
$$2V = a - 5$$
$$a = 2V + 5$$

　　(c)　
$$B = \tfrac{1}{3}a + c$$
$$B - c = \tfrac{1}{3}a$$
$$a = 3(B - c)$$

3 (a)
$$H = \tfrac{4}{5}a + c$$
$$H - c = \tfrac{4}{5}a$$
$$5(H - c) = 4a$$
$$a = \frac{5(H - c)}{4}$$

(b)
$$y = \tfrac{2}{3}a - 3$$
$$y + 3 = \tfrac{2}{3}a$$
$$3(y + 3) = 2a$$
$$a = \frac{3(y + 3)}{2}$$

4 (a) The standing charge is 200 pence and N leaflets cost an additional $5N$ pence.

(b)
$$C = 200 + 5N$$
$$C - 200 = 5N$$
$$N = \frac{C - 200}{5}$$

(c)
$$C = 400 + 3N$$
$$C - 400 = 3N$$
$$N = \frac{C - 400}{3}$$

(d) Scale A would give $\dfrac{(1000 - 200)}{5} = 160$ leaflets.

Scale B would give $\dfrac{(1000 - 400)}{3} = 200$ leaflets.

Scale B gives more leaflets for £10.

5E (a)
$$v = u + at$$
$$v - at = u$$
$$u = v - at$$

(b)
$$v = u + at$$
$$v - u = at$$
$$at = v - u$$
$$a = \frac{v - u}{t}$$

4.2 Inequalities

(a) If Kaljinder and Kaljeet spend £17 on hiring the boat for n hours, explain why $17 = 4n + 5$.

(b) For how long did they hire the boat?

(a) The cost is the standing charge plus the number of hours multiplied by the charge per hour, which can be written as £(5 + 4n) or £(4n + 5). If the cost is £17, then 4n + 5 = 17.

(b) The boat can be hired for 3 hours since 4 × 3 + 5 = 17.

(a) Can Andy and Bob hire the boat for:

    (i) 4 hours;   (ii) 5 hours;   (iii) 6 hours?

(b) Write down all the possible solutions to 4n + 5 ≤ 25, remembering that n can only be a whole number.

(d) Ron and Diana spend **more than** £30. Write down the inequality which describes this and give three possible values for n.

(a) (i) Yes   (ii) Yes   (iii) No

(b) The possible values are 1, 2, 3, 4 and 5.

(c) 4n + 5 > 30

The smallest possible value of n is 7; any values higher than this fit the inequality.

EXERCISE 2

1

2 (a) 4n + 20 ≤ 50

(b) 7 packs, since (4 × 7) + 20 < 50 and (4 × 8) + 20 > 50

3 (a)

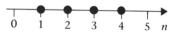

(b)

(c)

(d)

4 3·5n + 30 ≤ 60
The longest time is 8 hours.

5 (a) £35   (b) £10   (c) £6

85

4.3 Further inequalities

The solution to $6 - 2x = 12$ is $x = ^-3$.

Is $x < ^-3$ or $x > ^-3$ the solution to $6 - 2x < 12$?

$^-4$ is a number which is less than $^-3$.
If $x = ^-4$, then $6 - 2x = 14$, which is more than 12.

0 is a number which is more than $^-3$.
If x is 0, then $6 - 2x$ is 6, which is less than 12.

The solution is $x > ^-3$.

EXERCISE 3

1   If $x = 3$, then $2x + 1 = 7$, so the solution must be $x > 3$ or $x < 3$.

If $x = 0$, then $2x + 1 = 2$, so $x < 3$ is the solution.

(Check: $x = 4$ gives $2x + 1 = 9$, so $x > 3$ does not fit the inequality.)

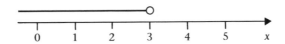

2   The inequality is '$2x + 1$ is less than or equal to 9', so the solution to $2x + 1 = 9$ must be included.

The solution to the inequality should be $x \le 4$.

3   The baking time is 25 minutes per pound plus 20 minutes.

4   (a) $x \le 12$ (b) $x \le 4$ (c) $x > 5$ (d) $x > 18$

5   (a) The basic inequality is $x < 3$. Other possibilities are:

$$2x < 6, \quad x + 1 < 4, \quad \tfrac{1}{2}x < 1 \cdot 5$$

(b) The basic inequality is $x \ge ^-1$. Other possibilities are:

$$2x \ge ^-2, \quad x + 3 \ge 2, \quad \tfrac{1}{2}x \ge ^-0 \cdot 5.$$

6   (a) The solution to $6s^2 = 150$ is $s^2 = 25$ or $s = 5$.
    The solution to the inequality is $s \le 5$.

(b) $s^2 \le 100$, so $s \le 10$

The inequality gives the lengths of the sides of cubes which can be covered with $600 \, \text{cm}^2$ of paper.

7   (a) $x > 3$ (b) $x \le 6$ (c) $x \ge 4$

4.4   Inequalities and graphs

Draw a number line and show the numbers of Joe's hamburgers which you can buy for £2 or less.

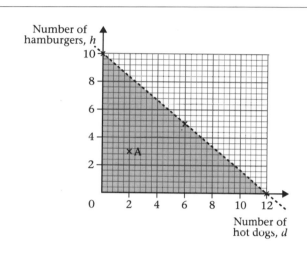

(a) Point A on the graph represents 2 hot dogs and 3 hamburgers. What is the cost of this combination?

(b) Write down the combinations given by the three points on the dotted line and work out the cost of each of them.

(c) What can you say about the costs of the combinations given by points below the dotted line?

(d) What is true about the costs of the combinations given by points above the line?

(a) The cost of 2 hot dogs and 3 hamburgers is £2·80.

(b) The combinations given by the points on the line are 10 hamburgers; 5 hamburgers and 6 hot dogs; 12 hot dogs. Each combination costs £6.

(c) The points below the line show combinations which cost less than £6.

(d) The points above the line show combinations which cost more than £6.

What is the inequality for the region above the line?

The inequality is $50d + 60h > 600$.

5 Non-linear graphs

5.2 Trial and improvement

> Plot the graph of $y = 2x^2 - 5x$ on a graph plotter and check that it looks like the graph shown above.

The graph should be a parabola which cuts the x-axis at $x = 0$ and $x = 2.5$.

EXERCISE 1

1 (a) 27·37   (b) 0·038   (c) 31·0   (d) 0·429

2

x	$2x^2 + x$ (to 2 d.p.)	Comment
3	21	x is more than 3
4	36	x is less than 4
3·5	28	x is less than 3·5
3·2	23·68	x is more than 3·2
3·3	25·08	x is less than 3·3
3·25	24·38	x is more than 3·25
3·28	24·80	x is more than 3·28
3·29	24·94	x is more than 3·29
3·295	25·01	x is less than 3·295

x is therefore 3·29 (to 2 d.p.).

3

x	$x^2 - 6x + 9$
4·4	1·96
4·5	2·25
4·45	2·1025

The solution to $x^2 - 6x + 9 = 2$ is between $x = 4.4$ and $x = 4.45$, so $x = 4.4$ (to 1 d.p.).

There is also another solution.

x	$x^2 - 6x + 9$
1·5	2·25
1·6	1·96
1·55	2·1025

The solution to $x^2 - 6x + 9 = 2$ is between $x = 1.55$ and $x = 1.6$, so the solution is $x = 1.6$ (to 1 d.p.).

5.3 Direct proportion

If 7 buns cost £2·38, how much would 3 cost?

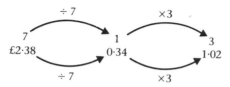

3 buns would cost £1·02.

EXERCISE 2

1 (a) *y* could be directly proportional to *x*.
      When *x* is doubled, *y* is doubled. When *x* is multiplied by 3, *y* is multiplied by 3.

   (b) *y* is not directly proportional to *x*.
      When *x* = 2, *y* = 6. So when *x* = 3 × 2 = 6, *y* should be 3 × 6 = 18.
      In fact *y* = 17 when *x* = 6.

   (c) *y* is not directly proportional to *x*.
      When *x* = 1, *y* = 4, but when *x* = 3 × 1 = 3, *y* is not 3 × 4 = 12.

   (d) *y* could be directly proportional to *x*.
      The graph through (0, 0) and (5, 2) is a straight line through the origin.

2 None of the graphs shows *y* ∝ *x* since the graphs in (a) and (c) do not pass through the origin and the graph in (b) is not a straight line.

3 (a) £(15 × 2½ + 20) = £57·50

   (b) 5 hours would cost £(15 × 5 + 20) = £95, which is not twice the charge for 2½ hours.
      The charge is not proportional to the time taken.

4 (a) The distance is directly proportional to the time. 60 miles take 1 hour, 120 miles take 2 hours and so on.

   (b) (i) (ii) and (iii)

Speed (m.p.h.)	60	40	30
Time (hours)	2	3	4

   (c) The time taken is not directly proportional to the speed. 120 miles at 30 m.p.h. take 4 hours, 120 miles at 60 m.p.h. take 2 hours. Doubling the speed halves, not doubles, the time.

5.4 Inverse proportion

> (a) (i) What does the graph of $xy = 48$ look like for negative values of x?
>
> (ii) Sketch the graph for both positive and negative values of x.
>
> (iii) Describe the symmetry of the graph.
>
> (b) Use a graph plotter to draw the graph of $y = \dfrac{48}{x}$ and check your answer to (a) (i). (Use the same scale on both axes.)
>
> (c) On the same axes draw the graphs of:
>
> (i) $y = \dfrac{24}{x}$ (ii) $y = \dfrac{12}{x}$ (iii) $y = \dfrac{6}{x}$ (iv) $y = \dfrac{1}{x}$

(a) (i) The graph is like that of $y = \dfrac{k}{x}$ (at the top of page 55), except that it is in the region where x and y are both negative. It goes through the points ($^-2$, $^-24$) and ($^-4$, $^-12$).

(ii), (iii) The graph has reflection symmetry with $y = x$ and $y = {}^-x$ as the mirror lines. It also has rotational symmetry of order 2 about the origin.

(b), (c) You should notice that all the graphs are similar to the one illustrated, with the graph of $y = \dfrac{1}{x}$ nearest to the axes and the graph of $y = \dfrac{48}{x}$ furthest away from the axes. The graphs have reflection symmetry with $y = x$ and $y = {}^-x$ as lines of symmetry and they have rotational symmetry of order 2 about the origin.

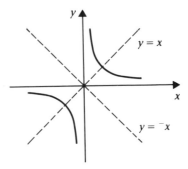

E X E R C I S E 3

1 (a) If 4 people take 9 days, 36 person-days of work are needed. So 6 people would take $36 \div 6 = 6$ days.

(b) To finish in 3 days, $36 \div 3 = 12$ people would be needed.

2 (a) Yes, since xy is always 60.

(b) No. In two sets of values, $xy = 26$ and in the third set, $xy = 24$.

3 (a) $xy = 30$, so $a = 30 \div 15 = 2$

(b) $xy = 7$, so $a = 7 \div 3.5 = 2$

(c) $xy = 24$, so $a = 24 \div 6 = 4$

(d) $xy = 45$, so $a = 45 \div 10 = 4 \cdot 5$

4 In questions like this it is easier if you first put the values in a table.

Frequency (Hz)	110	147
Length (m)	70	?

Frequency × length must always be $110 \times 70 = 7700$.
So, when frequency is 147, length is $7700 \div 147 = 52 \cdot 4$ cm (to 1 d.p.).

6 Brackets and indices

6.1 Using brackets

EXERCISE 1

1 (a) (i) $6(2a + l)$ (ii) $12a + 6l$

(b) $6(2a + l) = 6(24 + 30) = 6 \times 54 = 324$ cm
$12a + 6l = (12 \times 12) + (6 \times 30) = 144 + 180 = 324$ cm

2 (a) $6x + 8y$ (b) $6a + 4b + 8c$ (c) $12 + 6c + 9a$

3 (a) $2a + 8c + 6a + 3c = 8a + 11c$

(b) $6x + 9y + 2x + 4y = 8x + 13y$

4 (a) $V = \frac{4}{3}\pi(R^3 - r^3)$

(b) $\frac{4}{3}\pi(10^3 - 9 \cdot 5^3) \approx 597$ cm^3

5 The last three lines of the solution are:

$3x - 24 = 3$
$3x = 27$ (Add 24 to both sides.)
$x = 9$ (Divide both sides by 3.)

6 (a) $3(2x + 1) = 4x + 5$

$\qquad 6x + 3 = 4x + 5$ (Multiply out the bracket.)

$\qquad 2x + 3 = 5$ (Subtract $4x$ from both sides.)

$\qquad 2x = 2$ (Subtract 3 from both sides.)

$\qquad x = 1$ (Divide both sides by 2.)

(b) $7x - 4 = 2(x + 8)$

$\qquad 7x - 4 = 2x + 16$

$\qquad 5x - 4 = 16$ (Subtract $2x$ from both sides.)

$\qquad 5x = 20$ (Add 4 to both sides.)

$\qquad x = 4$ (Divide both sides by 5.)

(c) $3(x + 2) = 2x - 5$

$\qquad 3x + 6 = 2x - 5$

$\qquad x + 6 = {}^-5$ (Subtract $2x$ from both sides.)

$\qquad x = {}^-11$ (Subtract 6 from both sides.)

(d) $4(2x - 3) = 3(x + 7)$

$\qquad 8x - 12 = 3x + 21$

$\qquad 5x - 12 = 21$ (Subtract $3x$ from both sides.)

$\qquad 5x = 33$ (Add 12 to both sides.)

$\qquad x = 6 \cdot 6$ (Divide both sides by 5.)

7 (a) $a \times 3a = a \times 3 \times a$

These can be multiplied in any order and so:

$$a \times 3a = 3 \times a \times a = 3a^2$$

Similarly, $a \times 2b = a \times 2 \times b = 2 \times a \times b = 2ab$

Then $a(3a + 2b) = a \times 3a + a \times 2b = 3a^2 + 2ab$

(b) (i) $c^2 + cd$ (ii) $2c^2 + 3cd$ (iii) $2x^2 - 6xy$ (iv) $3cd - 2d^2$

6.2 Formulas and brackets

E X E R C I S E 2

1 (a) There are 16 pieces of wood of length p cm and 8 pieces of wood of length l cm, so the total length of wood (T) is $16p + 8l$.

(b) $\qquad T = 16p + 8l$

$\qquad T - 16p = 8l$ (Subtract $16p$ from both sides.)

$\qquad l = \dfrac{T - 16p}{8}$ (Divide both sides by 8.)

(b) If $p = 7$ and $T = 240$, $l = \dfrac{240 - (16 \times 7)}{8} = 16 \,\text{cm}$

2 The complete versions of the last two lines are:

$$\frac{2A}{h} = a + b$$ Divide both sides by h.

$$\frac{2A}{h} - a = b$$ Subtract a from both sides.

3 (a) $h = 3(x + b)$
  $\frac{1}{3}h = x + b$ (Divide both sides by 3.)
  $x = \frac{1}{3}h - b$ (Subtract b from both sides.)

(b) $y = \frac{1}{2}(3x - 2)$
  $2y = 3x - 2$ (Multiply both sides by 2.)
  $2y + 2 = 3x$ (Add 2 to both sides.)
  $x = \dfrac{2y + 2}{3}$ (Divide both sides by 3.)

4 (a) $y = 4(x + 3b)$
  $\frac{1}{4}y = x + 3b$
  $x = \frac{1}{4}y - 3b$

(b) $y = 4(x + 3b)$
  $\frac{1}{4}y = x + 3b$
  $\frac{1}{4}y - x = 3b$
  $b = \dfrac{\frac{1}{4}y - x}{3}$

6.3 Index form

> (a) What is the value of 3^4?
>
> (b) Work out the value of 4^5. (The answer is **not** 20!)

(a) $3^4 = 81$

(b) $4^5 = 4 \times 4 \times 4 \times 4 \times 4 = 1024$

> (a) Write down, in index form, 6 to the power of 3.
>
> (b) 'The base is 2 and the index number 5.' Write down the value of the number being described.

(a) 6^3

(b) $2^5 = 32$

(a) Find this key on your calculator.

If you key in $\boxed{2}$ $\boxed{x^y}$ $\boxed{3}$ the calculator will evaluate 2^3.

Do this and check that you get the answer 8.

(b) Use your calculator to evaluate:

(i) 4^6 (ii) 6^4 (iii) 2^8

(b) (i) 4096   (ii) 1296   (iii) 256

EXERCISE 3

1   (a) 4096   (b) 32768   (c) 6561   (d) 1771561

2   (a) (i) 243   (ii) 243

(b) (i) 64   (ii) 64   (iii) 64

(c) (i) 16384   (ii) 16384   (iii) 16384   (iv) 16384

3   From 2(c):
$$4^7 = 4^3 \times 4^4 = 4^5 \times 4^2 = 4^2 \times 4^2 \times 4^3$$
$$\text{and } 7 = 3+4 = 5+2 = 2+2+3$$

When multiplying numbers in index form, you add the indices (providing the numbers have the same base). The same rule works in 2(a) and (b).

Using this rule, $3^3 \times 3^5 = 3^8$, so $c = 8$.

4   Division is the opposite or **inverse** operation to multiplication and subtraction is the inverse operation to addition.

If you add the indices to multiply you would expect to subtract the indices to divide.
$$6^7 \div 6^3 = 6^{7-3} = 6^4$$

5   (a) $a^4 \times a^4 \times a^4 = a^{4+4+4} = a^{12}$

(b) (i) a^8 (ii) b^{16} (iii) x^{15}

(c) $(a^5)^6 = a^{5\times6} = a^{30}$

6.4   Rules of indices

EXERCISE 4

1   (a) p^8 (b) p^{12} (c) p^{10} (d) p^3 (e) p^3 (f) p^5

2   (a) $3^4 \times 3^6 = 3^{10}$

(b) $3^4 \times 4^2$ cannot be simplified because the base numbers are different.

(c) $(3^5)^3 = 3^{15}$

(d) $7^4 \div 6^3$ cannot be simplified because the base numbers are different.

(e) $4^6 \times 3^4$ cannot be simplified because the base numbers are different.

(f) $2^7 \div 2^3 = 2^4$

3 $a^2b^3 = 16 \times 125 = 2000$

4   (a) It does not matter in what order you multiply numbers so $cddcg = ccddg = c^2d^2g$.

(b) (i) ax^2 (ii) $a^2b^2c^2$ (iii) a^2b^3x

You could have put $a^2c^2b^2$ for (ii) and xb^3a^2 for (iii), but it is usual to write the terms in alphabetical order.

6.5   Factorising and indices

Explain why $x^2y + 3ax = x(xy + 3a)$.

$x(xy + 3a) = xxy + 3ax = x^2y + 3ax$

Factorise each of these expressions.

(a) $p^2q - 3pq$ (b) $p^2q + pq^2$ (c) $abc - bcd$

(d) $a^2x + abx$ (e) $2x^2y + 6xy$ (f) $a^2bc + ab^2c$

(a) $pq(p - 3)$ (b) $pq(p + q)$ (c) $bc(a - d)$

(d) $ax(a + b)$ (e) $2xy(x + 3)$ (f) $abc(a + b)$

6.6   More brackets

From the table opposite, explain why:

$(3x + 2)(4x + 3) = 12x^2 + 9x + 8x + 6$
$= 12x^2 + 17x + 6$

$\times$	$4x$	3
$3x$	$12x^2$	?
2	?	?

$3 \times 3x = 9x$; $2 \times 4x = 8x$ and $3 \times 2 = 6$, so $9x$, $8x$ and 6 replace the three question marks.

$12x^2 + 9x + 8x + 6$ simplifies to $12x^2 + 17x + 6$.

95

Write down simpler expressions for:

(a) $^-2x \times x$ (b) $^-3d \times ^-2d$ (c) $3 \times ^-2g$

(d) $^-3 \times 4y$ (e) $2c \times ^-5d$ (f) $^-5x \times ^-3$

(a) $^-2x^2$ (b) $6d^2$ (c) ^-6g (d) ^-12y (e) ^-10cd (f) $15x$

EXERCISE 5

1   (a) $(x + 2)(x + 3) = x^2 + 2x + 3x + 6$
$$= x^2 + 5x + 6$$

(b) $(2x + 3)(3x + 4) = 6x^2 + 9x + 8x + 12$
$$= 6x^2 + 17x + 12$$

(c) $(2a + 3)(a + 6) = 2a^2 + 3a + 12a + 18$
$$= 2a^2 + 15a + 18$$

2   (a) $(3a + 1)(a + 5) = 3a^2 + a + 15a + 5 = 3a^2 + 16a + 5$

(b) $(2n + 5)(3n + 2) = 6n^2 + 15n + 4n + 10 = 6n^2 + 19n + 10$

(c) $(4x + 2)(2x + 3) = 8x^2 + 4x + 12x + 6 = 8x^2 + 16x + 6$

3   (a) $(3x - 4)(x + 3) = 3x^2 - 4x + 9x - 12 = 3x^2 + 5x - 12$

(b) $(2x + 5)(3x - 2) = 6x^2 + 15x - 4x - 10 = 6x^2 + 11x - 10$

4

$\times$	$3x$	$^-4$
$2x$	$6x^2$	^-8x
$^-3$	^-9x	$^+12$

$(2x - 3)(3x - 4) = 6x^2 - 9x - 8x + 12$
$$= 6x^2 - 17x + 12$$

5   (a) $(3x - 4)(x - 3) = 3x^2 - 4x - 9x + 12 = 3x^2 - 13x + 12$

(b) $(2x - 5)(3x - 2) = 6x^2 - 15x - 4x + 10 = 6x^2 - 19x + 10$